LARRY M. BROOKS

authorHOUSE®

AuthorHouse™
1663 Liberty Drive
Bloomington, IN 47403
www.authorhouse.com
Phone: 1-800-839-8640

First published by AuthorHouse    11/07/2011

ISBN: 978-1-4670-7286-1 (sc)
ISBN: 978-1-4670-7285-4 (ebk)

Library of Congress Control Number: 2011919163

Printed in the United States of America

96

# DEFINED

There wasn't much confusion as far as who I was when I was growing up. It was cut-and-dry. I didn't experience much of the disorder that comes with not knowing who you were or not knowing what your purpose in life was. I knew exactly who I was, exactly who I wanted to be, and those two things defined me until the age of 16.

Prior to 1996, I hung my hat on my ambition. I was going to play basketball, and I was going to be respected; everything else circled around those two definitive things. I approached training for basketball and cultivating my fearlessness like it was my job. Basketball and my unflinching nature didn't shape my identity; Basketball and my unflinching nature became my identity.

Growing up in Liberty, Texas, I learned at an early age that there were only two things that people respected: athletic prowess and street credibility. Growing up in Liberty, all of my role models were athletes, hustlers, gladiator-type figures, or a combination of the three.

# THE BLUEPRINTS

Admirers would whisper and gawk at my uncle everywhere he went. D-Ray was among the elite. He was one of the most talented and recognized athletes in the state of Texas his senior year of high school. No matter where we went D-Ray would routinely receive special treatment. People would trip over themselves trying to rub elbows and converse with him. I saw firsthand the admiration his abilities brought him, and I wanted the same for myself. In my young eyes, he became a god. Someday I wanted people to revere me the same way they revered my uncle.

I can recall being 7 or 8 years old and attending countless of my uncle D-Ray's high school football games with my grandmother. We didn't miss many, and would even catch rides to get to the away games because my grandmother couldn't drive. My grandmother was the shy and timid type. The extra attention she garnered because of D-ray seemed to make her uneasy. When people would engage her in conversation she usually replied by ending the conversation in a polite, yet abrupt, fashion. No matter what the question, a typical response for my grandmother would be, "I don't know. I just pray to the lord and hope everything works out."

As my grandmother and I sat in the stands, unfamiliar white people would walk up to us and speak with her about my uncle. Random people would approach us, without introduction. They constantly remind my grandmother that D-Ray was the number one quarterback in the region and the top athlete in the state. The most intriguing thing to me was that these same white people, who were going out of their way to chat with my grandmother, were not talking to any other black people at the game. It became overwhelmingly evident to me that D-Ray's athleticism had not only elevated his standing in high school athletics, but it had also raised our family's status socially above others who looked like us and came from where we were from.

Grandma was uncomfortable when it came to being in the public eye, but her apple had fallen far from the tree. My uncle D-Ray was the complete opposite. D-Ray was a flamboyant, bigger-than-life character. The more his reputation grew, the bigger his character became. D-ray did everything "big." He spoke the loudest, dated the prettiest women, and basked in being the center of attention.

The fame and attention he craved was not undeserved; he had earned it. He had division one scholarship offers for football, basketball, and track and field. Colleges from around the country were jockeying for his attention. When D-Ray was in the neighborhood, it was like the ice cream man was coasting down the block on a hot summer's day. Everybody flocked around him, and everybody wanted some of what he had. In my eyes, he was the most famous and most loved person in the world. His life seemed destined for greatness.

Outside of the spotlight and away from the adoring crowds, D-Ray would revert back to being Donald Ray. Donald Ray was a dreamer. The only thing bigger and more impressive than his dreams was his heart. He genuinely loved his family and friends. Donald Ray would go out of his way to help a friend in need. At times he was benevolent to a fault. I admired how Donald Ray carried the neighborhood on his shoulders. His potential success gave everyone with a sense of pride, and more importantly, the hope that one of our own had a legitimate chance to make it big. D-Ray was egotistical, but Donald Ray was selfless. Donald Ray saw our people as his responsibility, and he brought us hope. It made me hope I could be like Donald Ray one day.

Along with the fame and athletic glory that a life like D-ray's offered, I also craved another type of respect. It was the type of respect reserved for the hustlers and thugs that I saw clash in the streets. They were treated like modern day gladiators when they were present on the block. I studied, admired, and emulated these men. Brian and John Bankhead were two of the most memorable from my neighborhood. Rumor had it they were my illegitimate uncles. My grandfather was dead, and his mouth was shut, but his secrets weren't dead. Their presence told his unpublished story.

The respect their peers had for them fascinated me. They did not make a lot of money, or have a lot of women, or dress particularly well. The Bankhead brothers' claim to fame was their expertise in pugilistic combat, or what we referred to as their "hand game." The Bankhead brothers were so quick to let hands fly that people instantly became nervous when they appeared. I perceived this fear of their presence as power.

Brian, the younger of the two, was only about four years older than me, so I got a bird's-eye view of how people reacted to him. When Brian was around, his peers were on guard. He had a reputation for sucker punching "violators" without provocation or evidence of any violation. The same power that I admired in him also caused me to harbor a strong dislike for him.

Brian had the habit of knocking out some of my peers that I happened to think were cool. He would beat down people from his own neighborhood for the slightest infringement. Brian was directly to blame for majority of the knotted foreheads, swollen and blackened eyes, and split lips I saw people walking around wearing. Much like the way D-Ray enjoyed the high of high school sports popularity, Brian relished in the power and attention he received from being a thug. I didn't care for his terrorist tactics, but the respect he acquired was irresistible.

The Huey brothers were similar in age to my uncle D-Ray. Since my uncle was usually busy year-round with sports, I had more opportunities to observe the Huey brothers operate in the streets.

When they were much younger, the Huey brothers would visit my grandmother's house and hang out with D-Ray. Many times they would stay overnight. We were maternally related, and our families migrated to Texas from Arkansas together. I was too young to remember if anything caused a rift in the relationship, but as they grew older, we saw less and less of them. It seems as if D-ray and the Huey brothers chose different paths; D-Ray pursued his talent for athletics, while the Huey brothers pursued the game in the streets.

Naturally, I gravitated toward the Huey brothers. They were flashy hustlers and were both of light complexions just like me. There were not many light-complexioned black males in my neighborhood. They resembled me more than anybody else, so I felt that they were the blueprint of a light-complexioned black man.

I didn't dwell on it publicly, but my complexion made me feel isolated and different. My father, my brother, all my cousins were all dark-skinned. It was all in my mind, but I didn't feel genuine because of my differences.

The oldest of Huey brothers, Steve, was making money, and he was making it fast. He had everything a young hustler could want: the finest women, nicest clothes, and a tricked-out truck. So few of the people around me had material wealth it didn't take much to impress me. Steve's tricked-out Nissan truck was the apple of my materialistic eye. He had it lowered with after-market rims and had a monster sound system. It was equipped with a couple of subwoofers that blasted his music throughout the neighborhood as he drove up and down the street. I could hear his truck approaching the neighborhood from what seemed like a mile away.

On hot summer days, Steve would park his freshly washed pickup across the street from my paternal grandmother's house. I would sit perched on porch steps watching Steve leaning on his truck and hobnobbing with folks in the street. Watching Steve would cause me to drift off and daydream that I was a hustler.

As I grew older my interest in basketball grew. Sometimes I would get lucky, and Steve would decide to play in one of the pickup games with the kids from the neighborhood. Most of our games took place on a makeshift court beside Mr. Dutchee's house. We would play two-on-two, and three-on-three depending on how many people were available. Usually an older guy would choose one or two of us younger guys to team up with him. Steve was as smooth on the court as he was in the streets. I learned how to finger roll watching Steve. He routinely picked me as one of his younger teammates, and I would always go all out in order to show my gratitude. I never wanted to disappoint him or be the reason we lost.

Steve's demeanor was constantly relaxed. I never saw him get upset or argue with anybody. People admired Steve not only because of his hustle, but because of how he hustled. He made it look good! Women and men alike wanted to hang around him. His swagger was so natural, and people were naturally drawn in. Steve was the man. Men wanted to be him, and women want to be with him.

Steve's eternally laid-back attitude might have been a survival adaptation. Steve's rail-thin physique made him look frail in comparison to his more sturdily built peers. If he had to resort to hand-to-hand combat in order to solve a problem, the odds were stacked against him. If confronted with violence, Steve was more likely to pull a gun or a knife than fight with his hands. The younger of the Huey brothers was known as being more of a fighter. Rumor had it that Steve was shot in the stomach after being mistaken for his younger brother. After a two or three weeks' recovery, Steve was back roaming the block as if he hadn't missed a beat. Taking a shot to the gut and bouncing back that quickly only captivated me even more.

I didn't know or see any college-educated men or business owners anywhere near where I was being raised. The people I had to emulate were the smooth hustlers, the roughneck brawlers, and the superstar athletes. I patterned myself after my surroundings. When choosing between the brawling Bankheads, hustling Hueys, and my uncle, I felt D-Ray's blueprint for success was the most suitable for me.

# DREAMS

A short time before my 13th birthday, I made the decision to focus on athletics. For two years, I prepared myself. I trained with the focus of a monk and the unrelenting drive of a machine. I had always practiced basketball and attempted to get better, but now I was taking my dreams seriously. I developed a plan. Every day included dribbling drills, hundreds of jump shots, and as many pickup games as I could find.

As an adolescent, I never spent much time living in one place; it always seemed like my younger brother and I were on the move. We bounced back and forth between living with my mother, my dad, and my two grandmothers. During a two-year period, I was enrolled in four different schools in three different states. Because we were always on the move, the opportunity to play organized basketball never presented itself. My game was restricted to the playground. That didn't deter me. Even without proper guidance and coaching, I did everything in my power to create my own blueprint to earning a college basketball scholarship.

Physically, I was limited, and that was my biggest obstacle. My stature was called small, skinny, scrawny, or boney. I heard it all. Personally, I preferred the term wiry. By the time I reached 16, I stood 5'7" and weighed in at an unintimidating 125 pounds. I wasn't blessed genetically with great size or natural speed. Those things I had no control over. What I could control was how hard I worked. My secret weapon was my work ethic. If I came across anyone who I felt bested me in any one skill set, I worked hours, and sometimes days, on that skill until I was convinced that I was no longer lacking.

One night I was watching a Houston Rockets game on TV and heard something that made a light bulb go off in my mind. As I watched the Rockets game an announcer mention how Sam Cassell was not as physically gifted as the other guards, but he somehow was clearly more than a match for them. For what he lacked in athleticism, he made up for by being smart and crafty. He could get to anywhere he wanted on the floor. I sat there and watched him dart and slash effortlessly thought the Orlando Magic defense. The announcer had just described what I could be if I worked hard enough. I set the VCR to record all of Sam Cassell's televised games. I would absorb his moves from the videotape and then rush to the basketball court to put them into practice. When I applied what I learned against competition, much to my disbelief, the moves actually worked. My new found success sparked an epiphany. Why stop with Sam Cassell? I began to search NBA games for the best of the best. Next I studied Glen Rice, the shooting ace from the Miami Heat. I wanted his jump shot. I continued to improve, and my confidence continued to grow.

I began the pursuit of my dreams with this seemingly simple formula: Work hard and focus on your goal, and everything will just fall into place. With my blueprint of a man and my head full dreams, I began my journey.

# MOVING AROUND

I enjoyed venturing out into the surrounding neighborhoods and gauging myself against strangers. Playing the guys in my neighborhood had become monotonous. We had played each other so much that we naturally memorized one another's strengths and weaknesses. I felt like a boxer who had beaten everyone in his gym. In order to challenge myself I needed to venture outside of the neighborhood and trade the comfort of familiarity for the test of unpredictability.

Playing pickup basketball games away from my neighborhood gave me an opportunity to hone my skills against a wide variety of competition. Traveling and meeting new people was amusing, but it did not come without danger. Though I learned countless lessons on the court, I learned even more in the pursuit of the game. One of the most important lessons I learned was the art of moving around alone while in hostile territory.

My bike was my primary source of transportation, and it enabled me to explore whatever city I happened to be living in at the time. I would ride my bike through different neighborhoods, searching for guys my age playing basketball. If I found a game and everything seemed kosher, I would join in and test my skills. My bike and I pedaled through projects, subdivisions, apartment complexes, and trailer parks. Because I was raised in rural community, I was somewhat naive when it came to my new surroundings. Back in Liberty, there were not many housing projects, and I had trouble distinguishing a housing project from an apartment complex. They all looked the same to me. Wandering unescorted into the projects was not the smartest or safest way to find new playmates.

I found that areas made up of primarily military families were safer and a lot less risky than the projects. These neighborhoods were filled with the stereotypical soccer moms who brought refreshments out to us between games like on TV. While I enjoyed Capri Suns and orange wedges just as much as the next kid, that environment just did not offer the type of competition that I was looking for. The best competition was back in the projects, but sometimes those games came with a price.

The majority of the time I would play ball in unfamiliar neighborhoods without incident. Exploring on my bike provided me the opportunity to meet a lot of new people. I became friends with people I would not have met had it not been for my exploration. Basketball was a common ground between many young, black men and was a natural icebreaker.

Just as easily as basketball brought new friends, it also made new enemies. On more than one occasion, I found myself in foreign territory alone and surrounded by hostiles. After a few unpleasant encounters, I began developing a sixth sense for when things were about to get ugly. I could feel trouble was looming, and I learned to sidestep a majority of the unfavorable situations.

Venturing into different neighborhoods, unaware of what awaited me, tested my testicular fortitude. These experiences built and fortified a special type of courage within me. I was not amongst friends; I was in the company of strangers. I understood the risk involved with randomly appearing in certain areas, but I enjoyed the challenge more than I feared possible consequences. Nine out of 10 times I would play without incident, but there was always that one time. That one time out of 10, for lack of better terms, I picked the wrong niggas to fuck with.

My exploits would sometimes provoke a physical confrontation with a local who did not care for my intrusion of his territory. I did not always end up on the winning side, but I began to cultivate a reputation and confidence in the streets. I never backed down from an altercation, no matter what the odds. If I was challenged, I swallowed my fear and engaged the challenger . . . in some cases, challengers. The more I fought, the less I feared confrontation.

Most people who approached me with animosity did not really want to get physical. They assumed because of my size, that bluffing would be enough to make me tuck my tail. I was no fool; getting stomped for no reason was not something I wanted to subject myself to. It was common knowledge that if you got into an altercation on somebody else's turf with no pass and no backup, things would not end nicely for you. That hood would represent by stomping a hole in your chest. There would be no one-on-one fisticuffs, and there would be no chance for victory.

Shortly after moving to Hinesville, Georgia, I found myself playing ball outside of Hinesville Middle School, or HMS as we called it. My mother was clueless that I would venture off on my bike for such long distances. She assumed I had enough sense to stay within a one-mile radius of our home. I habitually wandered three and four miles away from home in search of competition.

Outside of the middle school there were a couple of courts available to play alone. I decided to join a game of 21 with three boys in my age range. Their demeanor did not raise any red flags, and the games were competitive. There was one guy in particular who challenged me on offense and defense. He was slightly bigger and stronger than I was, but he was not as quick on his feet. The competition between he and I intensified as the games went on. I didn't sense any animosity, only competitiveness. After I won hand full of games, my competitors' actions caught me off guard and transformed the entire situation.

We were under the rim jostling for a rebound when my antagonist cocked back and hit me in the stomach with his elbow. It didn't hurt much, but the force made me double over in pain. He had caught me off guard. I glanced at him hoping to see that he was apologetic. All I found was an ashy-lipped smirk smeared across his face. His two friends stood, with their hands on their knees, convulsing with laughter. The situation was still manageable; I wasn't hurt, but I was fuming. The situation had become inhospitable unexpectedly, but I was not about to jump on my bike and ride off like a coward. I was going to finish the game and play the same way I had started. If they had any aspirations to jump me, they should have done it while my guard was down.

The game continued. I did not speak, and all friendliness had vacated from my appearance. I attempted to bait him into trying me again, but after the cowardly elbow, he shied away from playing me one-on-one. Still fuming, I searched for my opportunity to retaliate. Generally speaking, most children are raised to defend themselves against violence. Only if someone initiates it is it acceptable to use violence in retaliation without fear of facing punishment. In Liberty, we did not subscribe to that method of thinking. We were taught to be proactive. When faced with a situation that had the likelihood of becoming physical, I would swing first. That was the philosophy that I lived by. If a man, woman, or even an animal posed a potential physical threat, I had been given the green light to engage. In plain terms: It was acceptable to shoot first and ask questions later.

After the final game of 21 ended with my antagonist on the losing end, I was on full alert. I was not about to get caught off guard again. I knew that the two other boys were my counterpart's flunkies. This made it obvious that there was a good chance I would have to take on all three if I retaliated against the elbow thrower.

At the conclusion of the game, I walked off the court ever mindful of my angles and distance from the pack. I wasn't trying to get sucker punched. As I walked off the blacktop, I heard something that stopped me in my tracks.

"Punk-ass nigga. You acted like a Bitch when you got hit with that elbow!"

I turned to face the heckler, and to my surprise, it wasn't the elbow thrower provoking me. It was one of his flunkies, a tall, light-skinned, fake-thug-looking boy. Since he called me out, I decided to raise the ante with my reply.

"Fuck you, gay-ass bitch!" I then looked him in his eyes. "What you want to do?"

I knew my choice of words had just locked me into this one, and there would be no turning back. I squared my shoulders directly at the heckler but kept everybody in my line of sight. The leader of the pack who had initiated the situation did not speak, but he had a menacing smirk on his face. The second flunky did not say a word either, but he was there with them and therefore labeled a potential threat.

Earlier while we were still playing, a group of other children had begun their own game on the other side of the court. Once they caught an earful of our explicit back-and-forth, they encircled us in preparation for the throw down. When the boy called me out, I'm sure he did so with the expectations that I would keep it moving and ignore him altogether. I could tell by his reaction when I replied that he had not planned on getting physical. He had not considered the consequences of his words. He assumed that since the numbers were in his favor, that he could speak his mind. He was not prepared for the impending altercation, and I was not prepared to back down. With no chance of adult intervention, the skirmish would soon ensue.

After my reply, our back-and-forth banter intensified. As he spoke, he drifted toward me and slowly closed the distance between us. Before we engaged, he did the strangest thing. He bent down to tighten his shoestrings. He went to one knee nervously fidgeting with the tattered loops on his Nikes. It was a nervous reaction to buy time. His mouth had locked his ass into a fight he didn't really want. My previous experience in street fighting had taught me to be proactive in my approach. There was no dishonor in a preemptive strike. My only concern was the victory. After a fight, witnesses never spoke about who fought with the most honor. They only mentioned who got their ass whipped and who did the ass whipping. I preferred to be the latter.

Before the boy could stand up again, I quickly closed the remaining distance and hit him with a straight right to the mouth. That was his punishment for being reckless enough to drop his guard in front of me. There was more to come. He stumbled back like a drunken hobo, staring at me, eyes wide and watering. I locked in on him before he could regain balance. I unloaded on his face with as many punches as my skinny arms could throw. Much to my astonishment the boy did not attempt to throw a single punch my way. He closed his eyes and curled into the fetal position while I worked on him. Only a few seconds past before the inevitable happened: The cavalry came to his rescue.

I expected to fight all three of them, so I wasn't surprised when I felt the sting of someone's knuckles on the side of my face. The punch landed solidly, and I could feel the blood rush to the site of the damage as a knot began to form. Off balance from the blow, I halted my attack on the first boy in order to pinpoint my new aggressor. It was the instigator of it all that had just hit me. It was the same boy who started this confrontation by elbowing me under the rim.

Once again he had caught me off guard and then let up. He did not follow up after his sucker punch. He backed off and gave me the opportunity to regain my footing. I only had a second to regain my composure and square up with him. He and his cohorts were lined up abreast and were rapidly closing the distance between us. I kept my shoulders squared to all three the best that I could, but I could see that the numbers were not in my favor. If I didn't run, things could get ugly in a hurry.

In my mind, running from a fight is what cowards did, no matter the odds. Taking a coward's exit was not an option. So, I went on the defense and tried to keep all the action to my front. The second flunky hadn't seen any action. His eagerness to get involved prodded him to rush me. He ran at me and tried a jump kick. The kick was clumsy and, I easily brushed it aside. It didn't have a chance of landing, but it was enough of a distraction for him to land a punch to my mouth. I considered catching his leg and taking him to the ground, but that would have left me vulnerable to the getting stomped on. My only option was to try to keep the fight standing and remain defensive. No longer willing to fight me one at a time, the other two boys launched simultaneous attacks. Overwhelmed and outgunned, my situation began to look grimmer.

In the distance I heard a honking horn and the voices of adults but couldn't make out what they were saying. The three boys fled at the sound of their voices. I let out a deep sigh of relief. Then I gingerly picked up myself. The man who had been yelling from his car had gotten out. He walked up to me as I assessed my wounds.

"You all right, son? You need a ride home?"

"No, Sir, I don't need a ride I'm okay," I replied. I mounted my bike and began pedaling away.

As I pedaled away, I heard the man yell after me, "Aren't you scared those boys might catch you on your way home?"

"I will be alright," I snapped without turning my head or slowing down.

As I rolled away from the court, I pedaled slowly, leaning back, one hand on the handlebars. I wanted to show everyone watching I had no fear of a second round. Once out of sight, I shifted into overdrive, riding as fast as I could until I felt I was out of harm's way.

Once home, I did my best to avoid my mother. I could not let her see the bruises on my face. She knew that I often got into scuffles when I went wandering about. I just didn't want to run the risk of her finding out how far away from the house I'd ventured. If she found out, she would probably rein me in, restricting my ability to move around freely. While my scrapes and bruises healed, I avoided my mom like the plague. It actually wasn't much of a challenge. She worked long hours and was dead tired when she got home. She would never see my split lip or the big red knot on my head. I was still free to roam!

# ROOMMATES

It was becoming self-evident. The summer before my freshman year of high school my transformation from boy to man started accelerating. Starting high school would be my first taste of semi-adulthood, and with that came the responsibility of making choices that would help shape the rest of my life. My brother and I moved to Hinesville during the middle of my 8th grade year. My mother had granted my request to finish out the football season in Texas before moving us.

In Hinesville, my mother and stepdad were renting a three-bedroom, brick home. It was a castle compared to the two-bedroom trailer I had been living in the day before. To label the experience as a culture shock would be an understatement. I had never spent a night in a brick house, and subdivisions were a new concept all together.

Financially, my mother struck gold by marrying my stepdad. Literally one day I went from bouncing between my dad's two-bedroom trailer and my grandmother's small shotgun house to a three-bedroom, brick house with my own bedroom. During the 16-hour drive from Liberty to Hinesville, I daydreamed about how different the culture would be between my old neighborhood in Texas and this new life in Georgia. A change in subculture was nothing new to me or my brother. Being semi-military brats, we changed locations often. I was very aware I would have to adapt to the natives and fit in if I wanted to survive.

Traveling off and on with my mother afforded us the opportunity to experience living in a lot of different areas. Every place was different but still the same. There was a common factor with all the locations we had been. We always relocated from low-income housing to other low-income housing. In each new neighborhood, people spoke differently and dressed differently but were all poor so it never took long to assimilate. Hinesville was different. Hinesville was filled with the middle class—my first taste of the American dream.

The first 13 years of my life were spent sharing a bedroom, and even sometimes a bed, with either my younger brother or my uncle D-Ray or both. In Hinesville, I gained possession of my own room furnished with my own bed. This was a first in my life. My first night in the room was overwhelming. I got in the middle of the queen-size bed, spread my arms and legs as far as they could reach, and just laid there. I spent the rest of the night staring up at the ceiling fan until I drifted off to sleep.

Families in Liberty were large, and living space was scarce. Most of the boys in my age range shared a room with at least one other person. Some of my more unfortunate cousins didn't have beds or bedrooms at all. They had to make do with sleeping on a sofa pullout in the living room. Being blessed with my own bed and bedroom was surreal.

Having my own space wasn't the top benefit to possessing a single occupancy; I was ecstatic to be freed from defending myself against the crazy sleeping patterns of my brother and uncle. My brother slept like a wild man. I would constantly have to punch his ribs throughout the night to keep him from rolling around, kicking, and knocking me out of the bed. When I lived with my grandmother, I shared a bed with my uncle D-Ray. Sharing a room with D-Ray had been a life-altering experience, in both good and bad ways. Friday nights were what I lived for when sharing a room with D-Ray. D-Ray would arrive home late night early morning from partying and wake me up to tell me tales of his escapades. He would almost wake the entire house as he stumbled through our bedroom door.

"Nef-few! Nef-few! Get yo' ass up!" Then he would plop down in the bed with all his weight and damn near bounce me out the bed and onto the floor. "Pretty Doug has to tell you what happened tonight."

D-Ray was nine years older than me, so his role in my life was closer to an older brother than an uncle. Having D-Ray as older brother came with a lot of perks beyond the fact he was local celebrity because of football. From before I could remember D-Ray would do his best to expose me to realities of the cold world I would have to engage one day as a man. During our late-night conversations, he would tell me everything he experienced, be it good or bad. D-Ray littered my brain with tales of groupie love, sports triumphs and failures, and my preferred tales of alcohol-fueled parties.

D-Ray didn't limit my exposure to his world only to story time. There were a few occasions when D-ray snuck me out of the house to show me firsthand what the world had to offer. While I was in his care he wouldn't alter his life style or try to sugar coat anything. He would show me his world as it was. If he wanted to go to a bar or a hole in the wall club, he'd take me right along with him. I couldn't enter the establishments, but I would wander around outside for hours until he came out. If his destination was a house party, he would let me enter with him. After a few minutes he would hand me a beer and introduce me to all his friends as if I were someone worth meeting. Countless hours of my time with D-Ray were spent sitting on strange women's couches while they disappeared into a back room. After we left the strange women's house, it wouldn't be unusual for us to head right over to his girlfriend's parents' house and spend the rest of the night hanging out there.

Donald Ray and his alter-ego D-Ray played large roles in the calibration of my personal compass. Subconsciously, I tried to pattern how I would live based on what I admired and detested about him. He was the blueprint.

A lot of nights in my grandmother's house I spent lying in the bed wide awake. I would be too anxious to sleep. Instead, I would just wait up for D-Ray to get home and fill my head with stories of the wild world of women, sex, and alcohol. Because of my fondness of his lifestyle, the greater part of the time I relished sharing a room with my uncle. Listening to his adventures was the highlight of my week even when he passed out halfway through his stories.

There were drawbacks to sharing a full-size bed with a 6'2", 200-pound man-child: He didn't have to respect my personal space. Habitually, D-Ray would pass out and throw his arms across the bed as if he was in the full-size bed by himself. More times than not, one of his arms would land across my neck or back, and I would be pinned under the deadweight of his muscles with my air supply restricted. I would spend what felt like hours confined under biceps gasping for air until he moved again. The punching technique I used to control my brother didn't work on D-Ray. First off, I was afraid to punch him, and secondly, he was usually half drunk. When he had been drinking he could literally sleep through a hurricane, so punching him wouldn't have worked anyway. If sharing a room with my uncle became too much of a hassle, I would forfeit my rights to half of the bed. Instead, I would sleep on the floor beside the bed or in the living room on the couch. A lot of time the floor and couch were better options than getting crushed by a wild, flying arm or leg.

# THE WONDERFUL MIDDLE

In Hinesville I had my own room and my own bed, and the only thing I had to share was a bathroom with my brother. Life was good.

When I walked out the front door my first day in Hinesville, it was obvious I was in a new and exciting world. Everything was familiar, but different at the same time. In Texas, my cousins and I would hang a board on a tree, nail up a bicycle rim, and played on the grass until it turned to hard dirt. We considered that a top-notch basketball court. In ga, kids had backyard courts built on cement slabs with regulation-style rims and poles. I wasn't foreign to playing on non dirt courts, but nobody I grew up with in Texas had one in their backyard. There are always playgrounds with courts near apartment complexes and housing projects. As we traveled with my mother from base to base, one perk was access to apartment complex basketball courts. Having access to blacktop courts outside my apartment always eased the anxiety of moving. Housing projects always had plenty of kids to play with and blacktops to play on.

From my perspective, the housing projects we had lived in while traveling with my mother were an upgrade over living in the country. Living in apartments was a rare occurrence. I had spent majority of my life growing up on

Wallaceville Road in Liberty. That meant dirt courts were the norm. To live in Hinesville was surreal.

The move from Texas to Georgia wasn't quite as dramatic as going from the outhouse to the penthouse. But in my young mind it was damned close. The first observation of the new city amazed me. Most of these prospering people I saw looked like my parents, and their kids looked like me. It was amazing to see so many minority families living above the poverty line. Before Hinesville, I truly hadn't had any exposure to the black middle-class family beyond what I saw on *The Cosby Show*. Since I had never seen one up close, I wasn't sure the black middle class truly existed. From what I understood of the world, there were only a few types of black people. Black people were poor and country like me, poor and city like I saw on TV, or black people were rich entertainers. There was no in-between for us—only the have and have-nots.

Day one in the new world, I found out *The Cosby Show* middle-class lifestyle was not a myth. It existed right in tiny Hinesville, Georgia. Everyone in Hinesville drove nice cars, wore designer clothes, and ate the finest foods . . . at least from my perspective.

It could have been the newness of the move, but at first glance, everything in Hinesville seemed nicer. The weather even seemed more pleasant in Hinesville. The sun didn't punish you for daring to come outside before dusk in Georgia like it did in Texas. It was hot, but there always seemed to be a cool breeze blowing.

Hinesville wasn't purely a mecca for blacks. There were lots white families doing just as well, and better, than a lot of the black people I saw. But that wasn't a shock;

white families doing well was a norm in every town I had experienced. White families doing well was the image portrayed on TV, so I grew up thinking all white people lived in the middle class or better.

Rather white or black there was a common denominator amongst all the families that appeared to be getting ahead. Most of these families prospering had an affiliation with the U.S. Army in some form or fashion.

# OLD HABITS

To my surprise, my assimilation to suburban, middle-class living was fast paced. There wasn't the huge culture gap between my peers and us as I had expected. I anticipated and feared a difficult transition, but after a few minor tweaks, I quickly started to fit in.

Most of the tweaks I had to make to fit in were cosmetic. The first tweak was to change my outdated hair style. I had the classic high-top fade which hadn't completely faded out. The problem was I had been growing the long plait of hair from the back of my head for two years. I needed to eighty-six my ducktail. It was a dead giveaway that I was behind the times. Secondly, I had to convince my mother to buy my brother and me more fashionable clothes. Our wardrobe of wranglers and white t-shirts was drawing too much attention at school. In Texas, owning two pair of Wranglers and four t-shirts was good enough to get you through the entire school year. That setup wasn't going to fly in Hinesville. My second day of school in Hinesville I was given a fashion lesson as I walked to a class. A female noticed the Wrangler tag on my jeans as I made my way to my destination. She immediately proceeded to pull up my shirt and point out the label on my jeans to everybody in earshot. Her loud talking and clowning quickly created a scene. Before I could react, a crowd gathered around me had a good laugh at my expense. Getting laughed and becoming a person who got clowned wasn't something I was going to make a habit of.

Cutting my hair was within my control, but it was an impossible task convincing my mother trendier clothes were a good investment. She was raised in Arkansas on a makeshift farm and couldn't grasp the importance of trendy clothes. What I was failing to get her to understand was she was choosing to send us to school in middle-class America dressed like we were still living in low-income housing. If she was broke and couldn't afford to improve our situation I would have understood, but I knew my stepfather had money. He told me and anybody who would listen he did every chance he got.

Every school morning started the same. It stressed me to go into my closet and stare at the same two or three pairs of jeans and five or six t-shirts. Stressing about what clothes to wear had never happen to me in Texas.

As I stood at the top of a street waiting on the bus with the rest of the neighborhood kids I would secretly scan and admire their wardrobes. I wanted to own a Starter jacket and the same Hi-Tech boots the neighboring kids possessed. Even the kids from the projects who rode the same school bus had better threads than my brother and me. Everyone around us seemed so stylish and my brother and I were stuck rocking Wal-Mart's finest.

I had been oblivious to fashion until I moved to Hinesville, and I still didn't care too much for fashion. I didn't have aspirations to be the best dressed kid in school, but I hated blatantly sticking out, especially in a bad way.

After a few debates with my mother over clothes, I gave up. My mother wouldn't budge on the issue of brining us up to speed with our clothes, so I took matters into my own hands. I walked into a mom-and-pops pizza parlor and convinced the manager to give me a job delivering coupons door-to-door. I was only a few months from the age of 14, but I was an old soul when it came to creating a hustle. I had been poor, but I had never been broke. When I was 5, I started picking cans and bottles out of people's trash to sell. Getting my own money was and old habit. I wouldn't beg my mama or anybody else for anything again. After I started getting paid from the pizza spot, I started buying my own clothes. Keeping up with my peers wasn't a huge concern of mine, but looking out of place was unacceptable. I had my own money, so the problem was solved.

Outside of the normal stresses of school, my life was carefree. There wasn't any tension between the other neighborhood boys and me. My brother and I blended right in and made friends quickly. I hadn't made any enemies, but my mother had a little foresight on how I would react if a conflict arose in my new environment. Preemptively, she took away my pellet rifle and my air pistol during the first week. This didn't go over well with me. Shooting at aluminum cans was one of my favorite pastimes. "Safety precautions" was the reason cited as she informed my brother and me that she would be confiscating our weapons.

After she took my BB guns, she informed me of another problem she had with my country ways. She informed me there would be changes if I wanted to continue going outside to play. I would be wearing shoes every single time I stepped foot out her front door. Contrary to her belief, I didn't have a problem wearing shoes outside. My problem was I only possessed two pairs of shoes: one for school and one for church. Getting new tennis shoes for school was a once-in-six-months occurrence, so I didn't want to run the risk of ruining my shoes by playing in them. I preferred to play around the neighborhood barefooted the same as I did in the country. Going barefoot limited the wear and tear on my school shoes. If my school shoes got scuffed up, I would be stuck wearing flawed shoes for months.

I wasn't sure if my walking around the suburbs barefooted embarrassed her, or if she was simply attempting to protect me from embarrassing myself. I resisted the new rule on wearing shoes for as long as I could. On a couple occasions, she would pull into the neighborhood from work early and catch me outside shoeless and playing with other kids. The sight of me running around in the subdivision shoeless would turn her face oxblood red. After a couple of gentle warnings, one afternoon my mother returned home from work early and caught me out without shoes for the last time. I attempted to ignore the fact she had caught me slipping. Figuring she would just drive by and continue home and deal with me later, I carried on with what my associates and I had going on. As she drove by she suddenly stopped, rolled down her window, and screamed my name.

"Monte'!" As I turned to face her she signaled for me to come to her car door. "If you don't take yo' ass in the house and put on some shoes!"

She whispered through her clinched teeth as she stared a hole through my face. When she had that look on her face, there was little room for error. I was for sure she was about to hit me and embarrass me. She didn't, but I knew the next time I got caught she would probably get physical with me on the spot. I didn't think anything of being barefooted around these new people, but the reactions I got when she caught me outside barefooted was enough for me to break the old habit.

# THE PROTOCOL

By the time we arrived in Hinesville, basketball season was already underway. Once again I had missed a shot at trying out for a school team. The previous two school years had been split up bouncing between Texas and Colorado Springs, Colorado. Since I had moved so much, I missed tryouts the previous two years, and this would make the third year. I would have to wait to learn if had the skills to earn a spot on a school team yet again. There were major drawbacks to missing three years of tryouts. It bothered me that I would have to wait another full year to attempt to be a member of a school team. Each year I missed out establishing myself meant the competition would get stiffer and stiffer. There was no use of complaining. I did my usual thing and started searching for pickup games.

There was a bright side of my searching through different neighborhoods for pickup games. I got a chance to play against and meet a lot of the guys who played on the middle school team that I would have tried out for. After gauging myself against some of the competition, my confidence grew. From what I gathered, I was at the same skill level or better than majority of the guys I encountered. There wouldn't be a problem making the ninth grade team at Bradwell Institute the next year.

After a few months in Georgia, my mother decided she wanted to make Hinesville her permanent home. She quickly started the process of designing and building her own home a few miles away in a new subdivision.

There were two problems I had with her new plan. First, I was under the impression we were only going to be in Hinesville for a year or two years at the most. We were only supposed to stay in Hinesville long enough for her to finish her military contract out at Ft. Stewart. When she got out of the Army, the initial plan was to relocate to Atlanta. The prospect of living in Atlanta was one of the motivating factors for me to move to Georgia and not finish school in Texas. The second problem was more consequential than the prospect of not moving to Atlanta. Where she planned on building her new home was in a different school zone. That meant I would be enrolled in a different high school than the people I had met and befriended in the first subdivision. I was just getting comfortable when it was time to start over again. That would be four school systems in three states in three years. The thought of starting over again that soon wasn't amusing. High school was an intimidating undertaking on its own, and the new development made it an even more daunting situation. I would have to enter high school not knowing a single soul. My mother had pulled a fast one on me, but summer was close, and that eased my mind.

A week after the school year came to an end, we moved into the new house. The process of assimilation started once again. After so much practice, the "new guy" protocol was becoming second nature; I knew how the events at the new school would play out, and could set my watch to it. Girls would choose me, haters would hate on me, and then I would prove myself to anybody who had questions. I would have to make an example out of somebody to keep from catching new guy hell. I knew after the new guy protocol was complete the tensions would ease, and I could blend in.

There were some pluses to the move. The new neighborhood was bigger, and our new house was more extravagant than the previous. Half the houses in the new neighborhood were still empty, and that indicated there would be new families moving in periodically. New families meant new children. That translated to my not having to bear the burden of being the only new guy on the block for long.

Our new house was custom built. It was all-brick and sat on a half-acre lot. My stepdad, Timmy V, spent most of his time out of the country working and making the money he like to tell me about. For that reason, my mother was free to pick and plan the purchase as she pleased. She had taken the floor plans and revamped them to be sure every detail was up to her standards. Initially, it felt like a weird dream to wake up in that house. I had just gotten used to living in the other house, and now we had a bigger and better one.

The first day in the new neighborhood I rode my bike around and scoped out the new scenery. I wanted to find out what the new place had to offer. After a few hours of riding around, I discovered the neighborhood was a utopia. It was custom built for a 13-year-old boy. There were half-finished houses up and down both sides of the street to explore. To an adventurous 13-year-old boy, an unfinished house looked like an amusement park with free admission. The neighborhood was littered with boys of similar age to my brother and me. Guys were continuously playing pickup games in the neighborhood from sun up to sun down. There also seemed to be young girls walking around everywhere I looked.

The guys playing the pickup games all seemed to be two or three years older than me judging by their size. Being smaller and younger wasn't going to stop me from eventually trying to participate in some games. I didn't approach any courts the first day. I was more concerned with feeling out my new surroundings and finding out where everything was. After I rode my bike around for awhile, I went back into the house to cool off and digest everything I had observed. No more than an hour after my long bike ride my doorbell rang. My mother answered the door, and I could hear her talking to what sounded like two young girls.

"Monte', it's for you!"

I thought to myself, "How could anybody be at the door for me, I didn't know anyone in the area and I didn't tell anybody from the old neighborhood where I was moving to?" When I approached the door, there stood two young giggling girls. I was timid and shy when it came to meeting new females so I wasn't quite sure of what to do. I was very found of girls, but had zero understanding of how to approach them. Young girls would even tell me that I was cute, but timidity compelled me to admire females from a distance.

After standing at the door way staring at each other for a moment I broke the awkward silence. "Hi!"

The two young females introduced themselves and inquired if I wanted to join them for a walk. Before they could complete the question, I headed off to my room to grab my shoes. My heart was beating a thousand times per minute. Getting chosen by one cute girl was an accomplishment, but I had two cute girls knocking on my door.

Both of the young girls were very attractive, but initially I wasn't sure of which of the pair was actually interested in me. It was as if they both were equally flirtatious. The proposition of two women choosing me simultaneously was uncharted territory, but I had picked up enough knowledge about womanizing from D-Ray to know to stay cool. I was nervous, but I emulated what I thought D-Ray would do in the situation. I was to never reveal my hand to a female until after she put her cards on the table first.

Between the two young females, one in particular did majority of the talking. That gave me the impression of her being the ringleader. She was short, with long hair and had a coke bottle figure. Her looks were only mediocre, but her figure made her very appealing. Her counterpart was tall, slim, had a short haircut with dark hazel eyes. She wasn't as physically developed as her friend, but she was prettier, and her easy going demeanor made her more approachable.

We didn't waste much time standing around and getting acquainted. The shorter girl suggested we start walking in no direction in particular, and that's what we did. Slowly, we walked around the neighborhood and gave brief introductions of ourselves. As we walked, we passed by a few of the older guys I had seen earlier playing in pickup games. The girls spoke to the guys in passing and casually tried to introduce me, but my presence was barely recognized. There weren't any head nods, words exchanged, or any form of acknowledgement. It was beyond my understanding why I was getting a cold reception. The treatment was the complete opposite of my experience in the previous neighborhood. In Texas, a lack of acknowledgement was a show of disrespect. I assumed that the disrespectful natives thought I was soft or something along those lines. The scenario played out a couple more times with other groups of guys we passed by as we walked the neighborhood. I kept my thoughts to myself, but the disrespect was starting to get under my skin.

I knew what it was. Being the new guy had become second nature, and things were playing out like clockwork. The girls had chosen, and the haters had started hating. I knew what was coming next; it always happened the same way.

The constant moving around and isolated living in the country around only people related to me deprived of me of a lot of the social skills that were second nature to most kids my age. I hadn't spent much time hanging with girls that weren't related to me, so this was my first experience having girls as running mates. My social problems weren't limited to females. All the moving from place to place and living in isolation robbed me of the opportunity to be still long enough to develop any type of relationship with anybody outside of my immediate family. If we weren't bouncing state to state, my brother and I were bouncing from relative to relative. We would go from living with my mother to my father, from living with one of my grandmothers to the other, and mixed in there short stints of living with my Aunt Peggy. Change had become the only constant in my world. I didn't expect to be anywhere for too long. It was a waste of time memorizing names or getting too close with people who didn't have blood ties to me. All the moving around dictated that I gravitate towards the safety and familiarity of family bonds or solitude.

At the ripe old age of 13, securing a traditional girlfriend was something I still hadn't accomplished. I had experienced a fair amount of interaction with girls but I had never established any bonds. On a few occasions I was afforded the opportunity to make out with a couple fast girls. I had even gone as far as to have a sexual encounter, but bonding and making emotional attachments was still foreign. I started to think I should try something different.

During my first few encounters with the girls I didn't initiate any of the activities we engaged in. They were spontaneous, adventurous, and I enjoyed following their lead. Hanging out with the girls was a blast. Majority of our time together was spent exploring the neighboring woods and neighborhoods. We would hike in the woods around the subdivision, through the country club, back and forth across their golf course, and sometimes into town. Hanging with the two females supplied me with more than enough companionship, but after two or three days, the girls introduced me to two boys my age. Their names were Andre and Keric. They lived just a few houses down the street in the same subdivision. Keric and Andre shared many of the same interests as I did, so naturally I started hanging out with them more and more frequently.

When the girls first appeared on my doorstep a few days earlier, my first thoughts had nothing to do with the forming of possible friendships. Females becoming genuine friends hadn't occurred to me. From what I learned from D-Ray, girls were not made for befriending.

Before meeting the two young girls the only benefit of hanging with females I could conceive was the possibility of getting a chance to cut my teeth. After hanging out with them for a few days my perception of the two females started changing. The men I grew up with didn't hang with females. They ran the streets with their boys and dealt with females after business hours. I had never had the opportunity to get familiar with females beyond the surface level. I had only been taught they were a means to an end, the end being sex.

After spending countless hours exploring the world with the two females a few things became blatantly apparent. I came to the realization that I actually enjoyed their friendship, and that physical attraction and friendship couldn't live in harmony in my world.

Staring at the two girls hour after hour was starting to become too much for my young mind handle. I began to not only want to take things to another level with one of them, but also to take things to another level with both of them more than anything else in the world. It became my only focus.

The more I hung out with them, the worst it got for me. During our hangout sessions my pubertal hormones would be driving me crazy. I did my best to appear to be there for the platonic relationships, but I knew I would jump at the first chance I got to be intimate with either one of them. As time passed, something made me gravitate toward the slim girl with the hazel eyes.

Hanging with them day in and day out was breaking me physically. The slightest exposure of flesh would send my mind to the dark side. The situation was unnatural for me. I was a starving young lion doing my best to buddy up with two young tender elks. It wasn't working. There was no way I could control all the sexual thoughts continuously running through my head. The girls played as if they were clueless about my suffering. They pretended as if their booty shorts and exposed cleavage wasn't torturing me. The more we hung out, the more comfortable and revealing their clothing became. It was obvious they were under the impression they had domesticated me. If they could have read my thoughts, they probably would have dressed in blankets around me.

Being young and naive, I honestly thought that the platonic arrangement could work. And it probably would have worked if the girls would have stayed together as a pack when they dealt with me. The trouble started when the slim girl with the hazel eyes wandered away from the safety net of her friend's presence and dealt with me one-on-one.

After a week or so, the circumstances evolved. Things went from hanging out with two girls to courting one girl. The thick girl lived a few miles away, so she came around less and less often. The more I hung out alone with the slim girl, the prettier and more attractive I noticed she was. The thin girl had a golden-reddish complexion, beautiful hazel eyes, and she was easily one of the smartest females I had been in acquaintance with. I assumed she excelled in the class room. She spoke properly and habitually read books in her spare time. Book smarts she had an abundance of, but she was as naive as humanly possible when it came to the streets. Her lack of exposure to the world made her extremely curious and willing to try things she would have been better off avoiding.

Compared to my upbringing, I considered her rich. She had been raised in relative prosperity and was living the good life. She was living my fantasy, and I had been living hers. The grass always seems greener on the other side of the fence. Her family owned a sizeable house in a country club. Directly across the street from her home was a manicured golf course. Her family also owned another house in a different city. Two houses? That was unheard of in my world.

Our first couple of days hanging out alone went without a snag. We continued exploring all the hidden areas around us, and we innocently enjoy each other's company for hours at a time. It seemed like every day she would stop by my house and entice me to go for a walk or a hike. We would walk without a particular destination, hanging out from sunup to sundown. I never told her, but I looked forward to her ringing my doorbell and probably enjoyed hanging out together more than she did.

Ever so often we would switch it up and go on bike rides, but her coordination was so limited that bikes became a hindrance. One afternoon we were having one of our bike rides, and I had noticed she kept swerving off the sidewalk and onto the road. The road wasn't a major road but, it was busy enough to be dangerous. We rode in a single-file line because the sidewalk wasn't big enough for us to ride two abreast. We weren't more than a half mile from home before I saw her drift into the street one time too many.

Bang! A car hit her with its rearview mirror. The impact of the collision knocked her off the bike and threw her a couple feet. Luckily for her, she fell into a tall patch of grass. I was paralyzed with fear and judging by her face, she was terrified as well. We made the mistake of riding with traffic instead of against it. We never saw the car coming. Fortunately she wasn't hurt, just shaken.

The car that hit her immediately pulled over, and a man dressed in his Army fatigues frantically ran over to us.

"Are you ok?"

The soldier's voice trembled as the realization hit him that he'd just hit a kid. We were ignorant to the fact, but the accident was on him. Thinking as children, we assumed we were responsible for the accident. My friend and I both were terrified our actions would lead to us getting some type of punishment. But the soldier knew he shouldn't have been so close to us with his car. Unbeknownst to us, the soldier was just as startled as we were.

After the soldier confirmed his victim wasn't injured, he jumped in his car and sped off from the scene as fast as he could. He had just avoided a catastrophe. After that incident, we didn't ride bikes again. Walking was safer.

After a few weeks of spending every available hour together as platonic friends, everything changed in an instant, and our friendship never recovered. We were on one of our expeditions when she decided to cross an invisible line. After wandering a mile or two deep into the woods behind my subdivision we stumbled across an old railroad track. As we examined the railroad tracks and its surroundings, she reached in her pocket and pulled out some pennies and placed them on the track. She wanted to show me how flat a train could smash a penny. We waited and waited but no train ever came by. So we never got to see a train smash some coins.

While we were waiting she did something that changed the nature of our relationship. It caught me off guard because I wasn't confident enough to initiate anything other than us going for a walk. I was too timid to try anything physical. I knew how to deal with fast girls like I knew the back of my hand, but I was unsure about how to handle a female I actually cared about. I wasn't quite sure if we were strictly friends or if we were in the courting process. I had feelings for her and was physically attracted to her, but I wasn't brave enough to share my thoughts or make an aggressive move. My uncles had only taught me how to deal with loose broads and skeezers, but dealing with real women was what I would have to learn on my own.

While we were waiting on the train that would never come, she decided to do what I wasn't brave enough to do. She snuck a kiss. Subconsciously, I had been waiting on her to take action. Since she made the first move, my conscience was clear, and I could now do what I was trained to do. The kiss had my attention. Before I had a chance to react to the peck on my lips, she went all in with her tongue.

The fuse had been lit; there was no turning back for me. The kiss was like putting a drop of blood on a vampire's tongue. She was attempting to initiate an innocent boyfriend-girlfriend relationship. The kiss should have been harmless, but she had flipped my switch to the on position. Simultaneously, that flipped my mind to the off position. Instantly, I forgot about us being friends. Instantly, I forgot about all the time we invested in building our relationship. My hormones took control of every action afterwards, and my hormones didn't care that she was a person with feelings and needs. After that kiss we continued to hang out, but I always had something else brewing in the back of my mind. The kiss was nothing more than a catalyst.

Around the same time of the kiss, I started hanging out with Keric and Andre more and more. Keric was a ball of energy, and he was one of the few guys my age that was actually smaller. It was cool to be around somebody who understood the trials and tribulations of being substantially smaller than all others around you. Keric bounced around as if he was constantly amped on Red Bull energy drinks 10 years before the invention of Red Bull. Andre was a year older than Keric and me, and he came from a large family. He was laid-back and always seemed to be moving in slow motion. We all enjoyed being outside getting into stuff, so that's what we spent a lot time doing. We rode bikes through the surrounding neighborhoods, played basketball, and they introduced me to a lot of other boys in our age range.

One of the guys I met was Leonard. Leonard lived directly across the street from my house. He was one of the guys who hadn't spoken when I was walking up and down the street with the girls. There was no reason that he didn't speak; he just didn't. He turned out to be cool, but we didn't hang out much with Leonard too often that summer even though we were the same age. Leonard was busy running with a couple guys a few years older than us. The character of those boys he ran with raised a red flag with me. The older guys he ran with had a gangster façade, but they never engaged in gangster activities. I knew gangster when I saw gangster. I was raised up amongst real gangsters. I kept my distance from him while he hung with his older associates.

Every blue moon Leonard would join us in a pickup game. After one pickup game of basketball with Leonard one thing was painfully obvious: He was by far the best natural athlete I had come across. He ran the fastest, jumped the highest, and was naturally strong. Everyone around town was aware of his gifts, and there were always people coming through the neighborhood to sit on his porch and hang out. His house kept up a lot of traffic because he was already attracting male groupies before we set foot into high school.

# CONFLICTS

My friendship with the girl from around the corner was dying a quick death. As soon as I started meeting boys my age to run with, I consciously started the process of limiting our interactions. I didn't look forward to my doorbell ringing as much as I use to before I had male friends to hang out with. Slowly, I was cutting her off. When we did hang out, my mind was leaning more and more towards one thing, and kissing couldn't quench that type of thirst. My hands started exploring more and more territory. If she wanted to kiss, I used the opportunity to sneak a touch of one her modest breasts. If she let me get away with groping one of her breasts, I would try to feel up the other one. If I got away with foundling both breast, I would ease my hand up her shirt and rub a nipple. A nipple rub would usually get my hand slapped down. That was a small price to pay for progression.

Both of her parents worked away from home during the day. My mother worked during the day as well, but my stepdad worked from home half of the time and didn't have a set schedule. Her house was unoccupied, so we spent a lot of time there while her parents were at work. Hanging out at her parents' house gave me more than enough alone time with her to grope and dry hump her as much as I could stand. Kissing had become the ultimate way to distract her from my true intensions. She enjoyed kissing so I used it to my advantage. If I was patient and kissed on her long enough, I could slowly run my hand up her thigh. She would always knock my hand down or grab it before I could get too far. But before she could get control of that hand, my other hand always made a run under her shirt for a nipple. This cat-and-mouse game seemed to go on for hours and days at a time.

There wasn't much else to our relationship besides making out after that first kiss. All the walking around and innocent hanging out had all but died. It was replaced by hour-long make-out sessions. When she could actually pull me out of the streets from hanging with my new friends, my mind was always locked in on getting see how physical she would let me get.

One afternoon as I was enjoying cartoons and corn flakes with my brother she stopped by my house to see if I wanted to hang out. This time around her friend was with her. Two girls were always better than one even if only one had interest in me. Walking around with two females made me feel like a player. Other young boys who saw us out and about had to be sick with jealousy. Those new boys didn't have a single female to hang out with, and I had managed to secure two.

This particular hanging-out session turned out to be different. The thick friend of my girl had brought her boyfriend along to hang out with us. Coincidentally, I already had met him. I had ridden my bike through his neighborhood and played ball with him a few months back when I lived in the rental house. He lived about two or three miles from my new neighborhood and had ridden his bike over to see the thick girl.

After hanging out with them for a few hours I felt like I was sitting in a room with a pink elephant. They were light-years more sexually advanced than my girl and me, and they made sure it was known to us. The first sign of their advancement was their parading of their war wounds. The thick girl's boyfriend's back was covered with claw marks. He and his girl kept referring to how she had to dig her nails into him when they were getting busy.

They were more than aware my girl and I weren't sexually active. It was obvious they spoke on their experiences constantly to rub it in our faces. From their perspective, they were grown and we were still little kids engaging in kiddy behavior. If they had planned on making me feel jealous with all the talk and displays, they were doing a good job. Hanging with them heightened my urges to take my sexual relationship with my girl to the next level.

After hanging out a whole day with such an advanced couple, I started having the feeling that I was primitive in my sexual exploits. My counterpart was a much more sophisticated male. That didn't mesh well with my competitive nature.

My girl was innocent, naive, and easily misled when it came to anything away from school books. On the contrast her friend was very mature for her young age and I recognized she was the ring leader amongst us when we all hung out. My girl seemed to follow her lead like a little sister, and I followed my girl because she had what I wanted. If the thick girl thought getting physical was a good thing, then it wouldn't be long before my girl followed suit.

Life in the new neighborhood was turning out better than I had expected. I met some boys my age to hang with, and I had a girl on the verge of cracking. Life was just lovely. After living in the subdivision for a little more than a few weeks, hostility found me like clockwork. The girls had chosen. The haters hated when they saw me with the girls. Now it was time for somebody to test my testicles.

One sunny afternoon I was dribbling in the driveway killing time. My little brother was sitting in a lawn chair on the porch doing the same thing. It was the typical calm before the storm. In the distance, I caught a glimpse of two boys approaching. They were walking from down the street towards were Keric and Andre lived.

They were walking hard and fast like they had business to get to. They were too far away for me to make out their faces, but I could see their attire. They were dressed from head to toe in blue. Blue rags hung from their pockets. I knew what time it was. The two boys were definitely strangers and out of place in my neighborhood. My neighborhood didn't have any of that.

I was aware of their looming presence but it didn't raise a flag. I was in my yard minding my own business. There should have been no reason to be alarmed. But as soon as they got close enough for me to get a good look at them, I sensed there would be trouble. Either danger was attracted to me or I was attracted to it. I wasn't sure.

As the two teenagers approached, I concluded I had two options. One, I could nonchalantly walk in the garage, turn my back and not make eye contact. Two, I could stand my ground and look them in the eyes like a man. If I dodged an encounter with them they would sense a weakness in me. If they saw me as weak I would have to tuck my tail every time I saw them on the block. Showing unprovoked fear wasn't a legitimate option. I didn't have a beef with them. There was no reason to avoid them.

When they were in close enough range for me to look in their eyes that's exactly what I did. I didn't want trouble, I just wanted to acknowledge them and for them to do the same. It was all about respect. I demonstrated my respect by looking them both in their eyes. I gave the universal head nod as my greeting. One of the guys gave the nod back. The other guy just stared at me. When I sized him up he was clearly older, bigger, and stronger than I was. Even with the odds in his favor, I still wasn't going to let him punk me in my own yard. His glare was intimidating, but I held the stare with him. Stare downs usually didn't amount to anything. They were no more than a bluff game between males, and I was displaying my best bluff. There was one drawback with trying to pull off a bluff that I hadn't considered. What happens if he called my bluff?

The thug on the other end of my stare wasn't impressed with my bluff tactic. I had picked the wrong time to sell wolf tickets. My audacity to return his stare set in motion a chain reaction that I could not reverse. Within moments of our stare down, he proceeded to advance toward me straight through my front yard. I hadn't prepared for this. This wasn't really happening, was it?

As he made his approach, his comrade folded his arms and shook his head while he stared at me with a look of pity. The thug quickly approaching me wasn't like a lot of the adversaries I had locked horns with outside of Texas. He was the real deal. My poker face revealed no signs of fear, but I was scared shitless. The only thought present in my mind was, "What in the fuck have I gotten myself into?"

The sight of the extra large boy stomping through my yard caused the fight-or-flight response to kicked in. It was familiar sensation. I always got it before a confrontation. My palms began sweating, my heart started racing, and my pupils dilated from the anticipation of the skirmish. I don't know how I always found myself in this type of shit but I wasn't a stranger to unexplainable drama.

My bravado had once again written a check, and now it was time for my ass to cash it in. The odds of beating this boy one-on-one were slim to none, but handing over an easy victory wasn't going to happen. He would have to earn a win against me.

If I didn't think fast, I was sure the thug was going to give me a lop-sided beating in the middle of my own yard. He was closing the distance between us quickly. Before he could get close enough to engage me I created a diversion. Out of nowhere I launched the basketball I had been dribbling at his face. When he attempted to dodge the ball it left him off balance. The diversion worked, and I used the opportunity to move in and sucker punched him in the eye.

Out of my peripheral view I saw my brother take off running into the garage simultaneously as I charged in for the sucker punch. Subconsciously, I prayed he was going to call the police or do something that would help me out of my predicament. Who could blame him for ducking out? I had gotten myself into to this conflict by selling wolf tickets, and there was no need for us both to take an ass whipping. After I landed the sucker punch square in the eye of the thug, he immediately tried to grab hold of me. Luckily, I was able to break loose and stay away from his clutches. When he briefly had a hold of my arm I felt the drastic difference in our weight and power. His power unnerved me. He was so much bigger and stronger than me that I quickly realized there were only a few things I could do to keep from getting destroyed.

I told myself, "Okay, Monte. Keep swinging, keep your feet moving, and by all means, don't let this nigga grab you."

If he grabbed me and pinned me to the ground, things would get ugly. We exchanged punches at a disproportionate rate. I was quicker and had a more polished hand game, so I landed more punches. I was a natural fighter, but he was bigger and stronger. Every punch he threw had the potential to end the fight.

Here I was in the middle of my yard exchanging punches with a thug I had never seen before or spoken to for no apparent reason. Worse than having to fight a guy twice my size for no reason was the thought that there was no cavalry coming to rescue me. There was no crowd there to pull us apart, my brother had run off, and my enemy's companion was content with letting us fight until only one was left standing.

I could hear the other thug yelling and screaming at his boy, "Knock his ass out! Aw, I can't believe you're letting that little nigga stand toe-to-toe with you."

Time stood still and made it seem like we were fighting forever. I wasn't going to be able to stand my ground for too much longer. With each passing second I was becoming more fatigued from swinging and wrestling him off me. In a street fight, two minutes was a lifetime. During the initial portion of the fight I was quick and avoided all attempts by my counterpart to grab me. As I wore down, I became sloppy and had a mental lapse. As I fatigued, I abandoned my strategy of maintaining distance and moving my feet. It was a costly mistake because during the close-range fighting, he was finally able get both of his arms around me. He was locked on. After making a valiant attempt to struggle free from his bear hug, my heart sank. I was the pit bull caught in the bear's paws. I knew what was next for me. Suddenly, my feet lost contact with the ground. I felt myself being lifted higher and higher. Once he had me in the air, it was a quick and bone-chilling ride back to the ground. Before he plowed me into the dirt, I unsuccessfully tried to grab a hold of and lock up his arms to prevent him pummeling me once I was down. As I was plowed into the ground I felt all the wind vacate my body. I was done.

As I lay on the ground breathless, the punches started to rain in on my limp body and face. Before I too much damage was inflicted on me, the cavalry appeared! My brother Gene came charging and yelling into the mix from the garage. He was swinging a makeshift club. He single handedly managed to run two boys out of our yard.

To add insult to injury, on their way out my yard, my adversary punted my basketball up the street like it was a football. My heart was still racing, and I hadn't fully regained my breath, but I got off the ground and stood up next to my brother and his club. Again, I faced off with the two thugs. This time with my brother who was even smaller than me.

I should have known my brother had more heart than to run off and leave me to be demolished. Luckily for me, my younger brother had been there to rescue me from definite destruction. If he wouldn't have returned, who knows how things would have ended. My brother had earned my respect, and I was humbled by his courage and selflessness. We stood side by side in our yard and exchanged words with the boys while they stood in the street.

They didn't reenter the yard, and we didn't go out in the street. I was exhausted, sore, and scared from the encounter. There was no way I could go another round, but I didn't dare reveal my weaknesses. If he had known how tired and hurt I was he might have tried to finish me off. The irony of the thoughts I hid from my counterpart was there was little chance I would be tried again. My adversary was gasping for air and looked more exhausted than I felt. As I exchanged words with him it became obvious he couldn't go another round either. My testicles had returned, and I engaged in another stare down with him. I stared in his eyes as we exchanged words back and forth and didn't blink. I wanted him to know I was ready to do it all over again.

This time my bluff worked. The pair kept talking, but they also kept it moving up the street. Once they had walked up the street a bit the thug that had watch the scuffle picked up an old, 40-ounce bottle. He hurled it at us and watched it shatter on our driveway. I knew this run-in wouldn't be last time I was going to have a problem with him or his gang, and I was right. We crossed paths again a few months later.

That was the second time my brother had to join a fight with me since we had moved to Georgia. A few months before the latest incident, I had exchanged words with a boy my age in the North gate projects during a basketball game. I assumed the conflict was over and I left the projects without incident. A few hours later my doorbell rang unexpectedly. Adhering to my country ways, I opened the door without first checking to see who it was. Before I could get a good look at who was on the other side of the door, I was sucker punched in the mouth.

It was the boy I had exchanged words with from the projects. He had brought the beef to my front door. Without thinking, I charged out the front door and locked horns with him. What I wasn't aware of was he had brought two other young thugs with him. My brother heard the commotion and came running out of the house to join the three-on-one. Once the odds weren't overly in their favor, they ran off like some bitches through a hole in the fence that separated my subdivision from their housing projects.

My brother Gene was a year and two months younger than me. I was small for my age, and he was average size for his, so we were nearly physically identical. We had spent most of our lives without a man in the house. Since I was older, I naturally assumed the role as the protector and the disciplinary figure for my brother. I was older and felt it was my job to protect him. Ironically, he'd been the one coming to my rescue since we moved to Georgia.

A few days after my conflict with the thugs draped in blue, Keric and Andre rang my doorbell and asked me to join them to play ball at Andre's house on his driveway court. As we were walking down the street back toward Andre's house, I spotted a new kid on the block. He was standing in his front yard looking lost in his new environment. He wore the same look as I had when I first moved to the neighborhood. I remembered the guys pretending I was invisible as I was walking the neighborhood with the two young females, and I wasn't about to subject anybody to that same type of treatment.

"Hey, what's your name?"

He looked relieved that I had broken the ice and replied, "Nic."

Noticing him glance at the ball in my hand I opened the door for him to join our newly forming click. "We're about to go shoot ball. Come hang with us."

Since Nic and I were still both new and still outsiders, we began to hang out more frequently. We would engage in normal male teen age activities during most of the day but somehow our conversations always caused us to morph into the world's greatest teenage philosophers. We would chill on his back porch and discuss in great detail our interpretations of the world and the people around us. We analyzed any and every concept that crossed our minds. If there was a question, we debated it until we came up with an answer. We had the same philosophy of no gray areas. Every question had to have a solution. On any given afternoon we would formulate the answers to all the common problems that typically plagued a 14-year-old male and if we had time left over, we would find the answers for less pressing issues like world hunger.

# THE END CAME BEFORE THE BEGINNING

I received a phone call from my girl earlier than normal. She and her thick friend had put their heads together. They organized a day full of events that would monopolize my time for an entire day. The plan was for my girl and me to walk to the thick girl's house where she would join us, and then we would all head off to her boyfriend's house. Everything began without a hitch. I met up with my girl and headed toward the next destination.

The walk to her friend's house wasn't far. It was somewhere in the range of a mile and a half to two miles. The only snag in the plan was it was a blazing hot day in the summer. The heat was so intense that I started to rethink my decision go along with the plan. The simple two-mile hike had turned into a death march. I had never been to thick girl's house, so I didn't know what to expect. If I would have guessed on the thick girl's living situation, I would have guessed the thick girl lived in a similar situation to my girl or better. She was very pretentious and constantly comparing things to what she had or to what she was used to. Nothing was good enough or up to her standards. She constantly complained about everything.

Off first impressions alone, I assumed she was spoiled as a kid and lived in a world vastly different than mine.

After what seemed like 10 miles of slow cooking in the sun we finally arrived at our destination. What I saw through me off for a second. The subdivision wasn't anything like what I had expected. It wasn't that the subdivision was poor or beat up. It just didn't reflect how she carried herself. She had this holier-than-thou thing about her, and now I was clueless to whom this chick really was. Maybe her family was once well off and had fallen on bad times, but at this point, I could see she wasn't living better than anybody else.

Her house was modest and nothing flashy, but nothing to be embarrassed about. I was still naive and took a person's words for face value, but I had learned an early lesson about facades. From then on I would always keep an eye on those who overcompensate.

We stepped on the porch, rang the doorbell, and nothing happened. After about two minutes of waiting she opened the door and invited us inside. The fake broad had already started to work my nerve. What takes somebody two minutes to open the door? We had just walked about 30 minutes in the blazing sun, and she still wasn't ready. I wasn't stupid enough to say anything about it, though. The last thing I needed was to be kicked back outside in that heat. Besides, a ten-minute break was right what I needed to cool down anyway.

After she invited us in I stepped one foot into the house and then I stepped one foot out. Hanging out in that house was going to be a no go for me. First thing I saw upon entering the house were a bunch of family photos.

The ones that caught my attention were her dad's old military pictures and new pictures of him in cop attire. I also glanced over a cop uniform. It was neatly pressed and neatly hung from the back of a chair. The girls noticed me freeze up and assured me he wasn't home and wouldn't be home anytime soon. I was young but I wasn't stupid. I took my chances sitting on the curb, and being in that sun felt more comfortable than sitting on a sofa in a cop's house. I wasn't about to let her dad catch me in the house so he could put three or four rounds in me and say in the report that he thought I was an intruder. That's what I would have done if I were him and caught some strange boy laid up in my house with my daughter while I was out ducking bullets.

"Ain't this a bitch? This uppity ass loose broad's dad is a cop. This day keeps getting stranger," I thought to myself.

I sat outside on the curb across the street from the house and waited for the girls. At the time, the blazing sun seemed a tad bit safer than sitting on a sofa in a cop's house. To my surprise we were soon on our way. Before long, we had walked the few miles to her boyfriend's house and were ringing his doorbell. He came out and walked us into his home. We all sat in the living room and watched music videos. We weren't sitting down five minutes before I got the feeling that something was up. It immediately became obvious we hadn't walked all the way over there just to hang out. In fact, they all seemed to be on the same page about some secret to which I wasn't privy.

Before their asses hit the couch, the thick girl and her boyfriend were all over each other. They kissed and fondled and between sessions, one of the pair would glance over at us with a look that said we were lame for not following suit. I was into kissing and fondling, but I wasn't into public displays of affection on that level. I didn't see the logic in doing anything right in front of them. What was I to gain? I had learned my lesson about doing things like that in front of an audience and wasn't going to make the mistake again.

After a few minutes, the other couple realized we weren't going to make out with them watching, so they jumped off the couch and went to his bedroom. They shut the door, and that was that. I had been trying to take things to the next level with my girl for a few weeks, but it didn't seem like it was going to happen. Really, I was fine with that; I enjoyed the thrill of the hunt. What I didn't understand is why she would take me there just to make out when she knew what they would be doing. I watched her, and she seemed to be acting a little weird . . . like she had something on her mind or was keeping a secret. We were on the couch watching TV for what seemed liked two minutes when the bedroom door opened, and the couple came back out.

As we watched TV, I watched her simultaneously. She seemed to be acting a little weird like she had something on her mind. She was holding back a secret. We were on the couch watching TV for what seemed liked two minutes when the bedroom door opened back up. The sweaty couple stumbled back out the door looking very pleased with what they'd done.

The boyfriend stepped to me and told me to follow him to the kitchen; his girl approached my girl. My senses told me something was up and everybody knew what was going on but me. When we got in the kitchen, he held out his hand, opened his palm, and inside was one Trojan condom.

He smiled and said, "Don't worry about it. My girl has been talking to your girl, and today she's going to let you all take things to the next level."

I walked around the corner to see my girl with a look of nervousness on her face, yet she appeared relieved at the same time. I guess she was relieved she didn't have to tell me the plan herself, and nervous because she was about to cross a line with me. The entire trip had been set up for this moment, and everybody was in on it but me. It kind of made things feel cheap and unnatural, but it didn't matter to me at the moment.

As far as sex, I didn't have any principles established then, and I wasn't about to turn down an opportunity. My girl walked toward a guest bedroom, and I followed behind her and closed the door. That was my second sexual encounter at such a young age. It wasn't much better than the first.

After it was over, I don't remember talking to the girl or checking to see how she was doing. I got up and walked out of the room. I wasn't physically or mentally ready to cross that line with her, but turning down an opportunity wasn't something I was ready to do either. Sex was so rare that I thought to turn it down was foolish and cowardly. I had two shots in my first 14 years of life, and I didn't know when the next chance would come. That was my logic of the time.

She and I had never spoken about sex or how it would change things between us. I didn't know how she felt, but sex had a negative effect on me. I was so young that I didn't understand what we had done—the ramifications of the act or the new responsibility I had taken on. I had her virtue in the palm of my hand and didn't realize it.

My confusion was quickly replaced with a different feeling. Like a naïve youngster, the first thing I wanted to do was brag to my boys about how I had finally had sex with the girl from up the street. I wanted them to feel the same jealousy and envy I felt when I saw scratches on another boy's back. I knew that everyone I was hanging with was a virgin, and my story of conquering would only add to my building reputation. It never crossed my mind what would happen to the girl from up the street if I put our business in the street.

The next day when I was playing ball, I shared my story with a few trusted friends. I thought it would be a tale amongst us and that would be as far as it would go. Unfortunately, the story grew legs. I didn't know anybody and nobody knew me, but the story of the girl from up street being sexually active started bringing her all kinds of attention. We weren't an official couple, and we never even spoke on becoming one. That meant I had no rights to her, and she left out in the open.

My decision to share the story stirred the waters water around her, and it was only a matter of days before guys were coming out the woodwork to see how far they could get with her. I would walk by her house and two or three older guys would be sitting on her porch trying to put her bid in. Before our encounter, I was the only guy who paid her any attention. What we'd done brought her extra attention, and she wasn't mentally prepared to deal with it. She wasn't prepared to deal with me and how things between us were changing, and now all these older players were throwing game at her. Rumor had it that she gave in to the game of and older guy I didn't know shortly after being with me, and I hated her for it. By the time I realized I cared about her it was too late. She didn't belong to me anymore. She belonged to the sharks.

We only had sex that one time. We didn't speak much afterwards, and it quickly got to the point of us not speaking at all. I had lost respect for her after I heard the rumor of her sleeping with the other guy. At the same time, I felt it was my fault for putting her business in the street. At the time, I was too young to understand how I had compromised her virtue. After I crossed that line as a man her reputation was my responsibility, and I failed her.

I turned my back on the situation, and I put as much distance between us as possible. I didn't know what to say to her, and I couldn't look her in the face. I had betrayed her, and I felt she had betrayed me. That was the last time I would let a female get that close to me throughout high school. The little trust I had for females was gone, and I subconsciously turned myself into a monster. As hard as I was with men, I became just as hard with females. I treated everybody the same from that point going forward. I only wanted physical relationships and would disappear mentally and physically if anybody got too close to me.

# A SPIRIT STICK

Nearly a year before the incident with my pseudo girlfriend, I had been sitting in a class room in Liberty Middle School in Liberty, Texas. Like typical young males in Texas, I spent most of down time daydreaming about football games and football practice. It was football season, and in Texas football players were royalty. I wasn't the best player on the team, but I considered myself in the top three or four, so I enjoyed the spoils that came with that. Being a good football player on any level in Texas made life better. Football provided a set of built-in friends on the team, teachers gave you more leniencies in class, and being a football player gave me a sense of pride. My true passion was basketball, but football came naturally to me. I was fearless, and as kids, we played tackle football almost every single day in Liberty.

The memory plays in my head like it was yesterday. I was lost in a daydream sitting in class. That day I felt like I was on top of the world. I had finally arrived. I was finally on my way to becoming what I had saw D-Ray become. I wanted to be a Legend.

I remember daydreaming and sitting in class feeling like I was on top of the world. I had finally arrived and was finally on my way to becoming what I had saw D-Ray as. At that pep rally, I had received my first spirit stick from one of the cheerleaders, and that sent me straight to cloud nine. Every pep rally I would hold my breath when they gave them out praying that I would finally get one. After the last spirit stick was passed out I would get an empty feeling in my chest. The empty feeling would turn into a burning feeling. That burning feeling would turn into anger. My anger would cause me to want to work that much harder. It wasn't enough for me to be good; I wanted to be recognized. I needed to be celebrated.

The cheerleaders were at the games, so I couldn't figure why I wasn't getting any. In my mind, getting a spirit stick was like winning an Academy Award. I had finally gotten recognized for all my hard work on the field. During the pep rally earlier that day I almost went into shock when that cheerleader called me up to get that spirit stick. Life was good. School work was easy, I was good at what I was doing and other people finally recognized it. I wasn't feeling any pain. I don't remember what class it was, but I remember sitting there basking in my own glory and daydreaming of the greatness to come when my daydream was interrupted, and my life became infinitely more complicated.

"Te," she whispered.

I replied, "Yeah, what's up?" Then she dropped a bomb on me.

"Come to my house after the game, and I'll give you some."

I was 13, I was a virgin, and my hormones were out of control. Actually having an opportunity to have sex was like icing on the cake on my dream day. There was one problem with the proposition of sex, and it was that I didn't know how to have sex. I was clueless. I had a basic understanding of what I was supposed to do. I also had a basic understanding of how to drive car. Having a basic understanding didn't mean I was ready to get behind the wheel. I had humped and fondled every female that was naive enough to trust herself alone with me. I had also watched any porn I could get my hands on, so I knew what I was supposed to do. It's just actually having sex was a totally different animal. Having it thrown at me out of nowhere scared the hell out of me. How could things get any better? I sat there frozen in my thoughts and didn't respond to her offer. I guess she noticed I stalled.

"Come to my house after school if you ain't scared." She stared me in the eyes after she made that last comment. I could see she was checking for a sign of fear. It was felt just like we were standing toe to toe before a street fight.

I looked her right back in the eyes and I bluffed her. "Yeah, I'll come through."

After I responded I turned my head and pretended to go back to my day dreaming. That young hussy had just shaken up my whole world.

Outside I looked as if I was carefree and on top of the world, but inside I was a nervous wreck. It was game day, and my mind should have been focused with thoughts of football, but there was no room in my head anymore for football. My mind was completely filled with preparing for the sexual encounter to come, and I was scared to death. I had taken on every boy who had ever challenged me whether I was scared or not, and I would approach this situation no differently. By the law of the streets, I was obligated to handle my business because she'd chosen me.

I also figured if word got around that I had turned down a girl, I would look soft. I feared being thought of as soft more than I feared sex with the girl. I had no choice but to agree to her proposal.

It was always the same routine after every home game. The football team had to meet up for head count right after school ended, and then we were able to leave campus to go get something to eat. We had to be back on campus about an hour and a half before game time. That gave me about two hours to get to that girl's house and get back. The burden was too big for me to bear alone so, I told my cousin and my best friend, Big H, and a few other teammates of the proposal. Before I knew it, four boys and I were marching toward this girl's house for the showdown

Besides the fear of the unknown, I also felt excited. I was about lock up with this female and come out on the other side a man. As we walked toward her house, it felt the same as if I were marching to a street fight. The same gauntlet of emotions ran through my head: fear, excitement, and nervousness. I always second-guessed myself, but once I was committed to something, I had to see it through no matter what the consequences. This would be no different.

After a short walk, we finally arrived at the porch of the house. Reality hit me in the face like cold water. I knew I would be on my own once I got on the inside. This was a far as my support group could go with me. I stepped onto the porch alone, and I took one look back at my click before I rang the doorbell. They were pumped and cheering me, and I fed off all the gathered testosterone.

I got high off it, and I started to feel extra confident and invincible. I gave myself a quick pep talk.

"I'm Larry Brooks, the toughest and smartest nigga there is. I come from the hardest hood, was raised by the hardest niggas, and I've locked up with niggas twice my size and didn't bat an eye. I'm supposed to do this because this is what I was made to do."

I reached my hand out, rang the doorbell, and waited for destiny. After a few seconds, I heard someone asking who was at the door. It wasn't a young female's voice or a teenage boy. It was a grown man's voice. I replied my name, and to my surprise, her stepdad opened the door. He looked surprise to see me on his porch. The irony was I knew her stepdad. He was my cousin, and he grew up with my dad. They were running mates. I even had distant memories of my dad taking me by his house years before and the two of them getting drunk.

I exhaled because I thought I was saved from having to go through with it. Her stepdad was home and I was hoping he stuck around or ran me off, but I wasn't so lucky. He let me in the house, and I took a seat. He then called out to his stepdaughter and told her she had company. As soon as she came up front, he told her a few things and grabbed his hard hat and left for work.

As soon as her stepdad closed the door behind him she made it obvious we weren't about to play around. She grabbed my hand and led me straight down to the basement where her room was. As we headed down those stairs, all the confidence I had built up left my body like somebody punched me in the stomach and knocked out my wind. The first thing I saw when I got to her room was that it had windows that were at ground level looking down into the room. In one of the windows that didn't have a curtain was four young boys huddled together staring back at me and cheering me. My cousins and friends had ringside seats and were locked in for the main event.

With my folks looking through the window, I didn't feel comfortable getting totally naked with a bunch of boys watching, so we both got down to our underwear and jumped in her bed under the sheets. I had a basic understanding of what was supposed to go down, but things weren't going smoothly. I was nervous, and having the four guys clowning and cutting up outside the window wasn't helping me.

I fumbled around trying to get the condom on. I hadn't never put one on and never thought of taken time out to practice. It probably only took me a minute to get the condom on, but it seemed like a lifetime. I could tell the girl was losing patience with me, and that added to my stress level. I finally got the condom on and rolled over on top of the irritable girl. I'm not sure how long we wrestled around in that bed but after a few minutes, I ended the session and told her I had to go because we needed to get back to school and get ready for the game.

The walk back to school with was my friends felt surreal. For the most part, I was the first guy crossing that line, and they didn't know whether I had done a good job or not. They seemed like they were more excited and pumped up than I was. They bombarded me with questions about how it was and what was it like. I played the part and gave cliché answers. I don't remember the answers I gave. I only remember just wanting to get away from her house and get back to my life. I wanted things to go back to how it was before she crashed my party. The more I thought about what happen the more unsettled I became. I knew I had failed and that embarrassed me. My head was a mess and my pride had taken hit.

Failure made me feel confused and unconfident about myself. I wasn't comfortable with those emotions. I had never felt them that strongly before. Why did she have to interrupt my life? I felt myself getting angrier and angrier the more I thought. By game time I was in a full blown internal rage. During the game I flew all over the field. I didn't care if I hurt myself or hurt anybody with my wild play. I laid a couple hard late hits on the opposing quarterback and made a play on a running back behind the line of scrimmage from my strong safety position. I was way undersized for my position, but I always made up for it with my aggression. Today was different. I wasn't just aggressive; I was angry. I was so emotional I couldn't keep my breath.

After one series I remember walking back to the sideline. My coach was so pumped with my play he grabbed my helmet and shook it. He then slapped me on the ear. I was so out of it I couldn't understand or hear what he saying, but I could tell he was happy with me. A few plays later he stuck me in on offense at receiver which I played a few snaps a game. He called a pass play for me that we had practiced at a hundred times. It was a quick slant. I ran the route perfectly because it was second nature. But I was so pumped up on adrenaline my eyes were teary and I couldn't see the ball. Our quarterback threw a perfect pass that went right through both of my hands and hit me in the chest. I dropped the ball and then almost got killed by a linebacker.

Coach sent somebody in for me for the next play. I couldn't focus enough to play offense because I couldn't see. On defense, I didn't need focus to be effective. My anger was enough. After the game my teammates were giving me props about my conquests on and off the field, and it brought my confidence back up briefly. Maybe I had overreacted to my failure. Maybe I didn't do as badly as I thought. Maybe things had gone like they were supposed to.

The next day I saw the young hussy first thing when I got to campus. She saw me too and smiled. But I was so embarrassed about what had taken place the day before I pretended not see her and hit a quick U-turn. I didn't have the courage to face her, and that U-turn was the worst thing I could have done. I didn't know it then, but she took my avoidance of her as disrespect.

We had a class coming up together and there would be no avoiding that. I would deal with her then. I wasn't ready to look her in the eyes and deal with her opinion of me. I was a failure as a man. My friends didn't know it, but she did. Couldn't fake it with her, she knew the truth about me.

News about sex in junior high spread like a wild fire. Before the first class was over my experience the day before was on the tongue of every mouth I could see moving. It felt like everyone was staring at me and whispering. I didn't know if the talk was good or bad. There was nowhere to hide, and my imagination was running wild. Where they laughing at me or in awe? It didn't matter. The fear of being publicly humiliated started turning to anger. Everything always turned into anger. It wasn't my fault that all this was happening to me. I didn't initiate any of this. I placed blame on the girl for putting me in a situation I wasn't ready for. I blamed her for the embarrassment I was feeling. I felt played.

After first period was over I rushed toward the next class. I didn't want to spend any extra time in the hallways were people could see me. The next class I had was with the girl, and I was ready to get the confrontation over with. One thing I knew about this girl was that she was hood. She had a reputation of being a badass. She loved to fight and run her mouth because she whooped girls and boys alike. One reason she was so bold was because she had a crazy older brother. He was in and out of jail, and a lot of people gave her extra space because of the fear of and respect for him. I didn't have to worry about him. My hood was strong and he would have to go through 10 cats way harder than him to get to me if I did something to his sister.

Approaching the second period class I could see there was a crowd formed in front of where I was headed. Approaching second period I could see there was a crowd formed in front of where I was headed. Before I could get close enough to see what was going on, I could hear that crazy broad talking loud over the crowd. The crowd had gathered around her and she was assassinating my character the best she could.

"That nigga didn't know what the fuck he was doing. He couldn't even figure out how to get it in good."

My worst nightmare was happening in real life. I was so angry I couldn't see or think clearly. I felt my eyes water up, my throat dried and I could feel my heart pounding. The only thought I could come up with was to shut her ass down. I marched straight through the crowd and when she saw me, she smiled and looked me in the face as if to tell me she was purposely going to ruin me. She had underestimated me. She thought she was in for a battle of words, but I never exchanged words.

I didn't bother taking off my book bag. I punched her in the stomach as hard as I could. With my fist still stuck in her stomach I could hear her gasping for air. Her eyes instantly watered up. That was that. Her mouth was shut. Everything suddenly went quiet. The only thing I heard after I punched her was the crowd saying, "Ooh!" Nobody was expecting me to stoop as low as to punch a girl.

She doubled over, and I walked away and left her just like that. I walked into class took my bag off and sat down as if nothing had happened. After my adrenaline stopped pumping, reality hit. I had sunk to a new low. It felt worse than being embarrassed about my failure. What in the hell had I just done? I had let my emotions take control of me and made a horrible situation a worse one. Two days ago I was on top of the world. Now I was a failure at being a man and a girl beater. Everything was spiraling downward. How in the hell does life change so fast?

She entered class a few minutes later. She still had dried tear marks on her cheeks. She had failed to fully wipe them away. Glancing over at her made my soul sink even lower. My life was spinning and every decision I made was making it worse. This whole situation had put me in a bad place. This girl had tried to publicly assassinate my character and had destroyed my ego. Even with all that, I knew her situation was much worse than mine.

I wasn't totally sure of what she had been exposed to growing up, but I had heard the rumors. Knowing that I had added to her problems ate away at my conscience as we sat in that class. As I sat there, it dawned on me what happened. Sex wasn't just sex for her. She had attempted to open up and get my attention in the only way she knew how. Rumor had it that she had been having sex with a couple of her older brother's friends and had been doing it for a couple of years. Some of the sex probably wasn't by choice, and some was, but she was still only 13. The men in her circle were corrupt, and she had developed a twisted view of how to deal with men. Sitting beside her in silence ate away at me and continued to eat at me days and weeks afterward.

Football season ended three or four weeks after our incident, and I took my mother up on her offer. My brother and I moved to Hinesville. A year after the first Gulf War she had been stationed at Ft. Stewart, the military base adjacent to Hinesville. She had informed me that she would be there for a short spell and then she would head off to Atlanta. I had planned to wait out Hinesville and join her when she moved to Atlanta to avoid the additional relocation. Prior to that situation I had been torn about leaving Texas where I was established and facing the unknown again. My conscience ate at me about failing at sex and punching that girl. I was embarrassed and wanted to run away and hide. Hinesville was the perfect opportunity to get away. There really wasn't anything to think about anymore seeing as the scale had been tilted. Beyond wanting to duck out, I missed my mother. I hadn't seen much of her for a few years, and it was something that bothered me. It was the best way to kill two birds with one stone. ga was the move.

# INFECTION

I don't remember if I broke down and cried, but I remember lying in bed day after day feeling like an empty vessel. I didn't want to eat, didn't want to drink, and didn't want to share what was going on in my head. Who could understand what I was going through? I had never felt so isolated and alone. My life was an island and the world could keep spinning without me participating.

19'96 was in its beginning stages. I was a 16-year-old man having his first experience with the pain of letting go of a dream. The fire that ran through my body was slowly smoldering and dying a slow and painful death. For countless weeks afterwards it was the same thing every morning. I would wake up and realize a limb had been cut off my body. I needed to accept the fact it was gone so I could heal and move on with my life.

My mind was spiraling out of control. Anger, hate, resentment, fear, and confusion were felt all at once. My senses felt overwhelmed. My entire existence had been spent chasing one thing and it was all gone in one moment of weakness. In one moment I cracked and allowed another man's thoughts seep into my head and change my destiny.

The same scene replayed in my head over and over again. Should have done a hundred things differently and my life wouldn't be in this state. Now all I had to show for my life's work was a hundred questions. What was the purpose of all the time I had logged practicing? What did I have to show for my dedication? What would be my new purpose in life? Who am I? My life had been simple. For any question about my destiny, basketball had always been the answer.

With an extreme amount of prodding in a certain direction I had made a conscious decision to move a route with my life. I couldn't take full responsibility for the change in direction, but the consequences of living with the decision were mine alone to bear. Timmy V had provided enough consistent prodding of me in certain direction to manipulate my mind, but the choice was ultimately mine as a man. I had failed myself and allowed him direct me away from my dreams.

Prior to my mental break down, the biggest sporting event of the year in Hinesville had taken place. The aftereffect of my interaction with that event was a blow to my psyche that left me weak and open for infection. The big event was the annual basketball game between cross-town rivals Liberty County High and Bradwell Institute.

The game before the rival game earned me my first start on the varsity team. It was the game vs. Savannah High. The coach didn't bother to inform me I would be starting until we were on the bus en route to the game. The presentation of the opportunity totally caught me off guard. I had about an hour to get my mind adjusted to the opportunity that had fallen into my lap. I wasn't surprised that I got the starting nod because of anything that had to do with my physical skill. In my opinion, I had passed the varsity starting point guard in physical skill the year before while I was still playing JV.

The start came as a surprise because of my relationship with the head coach. Coach rarely spoke directly to me, and I wasn't sure he actually knew my name. Throughout my time on varsity and JV he called me by the wrong name more times than not. He had a habit of calling me "Fernando." Fernando was the other light-skinned guy on the team. Here was this man that couldn't get my name right handing me the keys to everything I had worked years to obtain. It felt surreal.

The year before I worked my way through the ranks of JV and moved up the depth chart. After being an unknown on the team, I was starting by the fourth game. Varsity was different. There didn't seem to be a method to the madness. The harder I worked, the more I improved. The more I improved, the less I played in games and the greater my frustration became.

On the outside looking in it appeared as if the coach only played people he knew for years and was familiar with. During tryouts, I witnessed him cut multiple guys that had more physical talent than half the people on the team because he wasn't comfortable with their appearance or background. Talent and hard work weren't completely overlooked, but politics played too big of a role in his approach for high school sports.

Timmy V noticed the blatant flaw in the coach from the first game he witnessed. He made sure I knew it day one. Timmy V never invested much time into fatherly activities like taking me or my brother to the park or helping me with homework, but he came to every game I played at home. He always showed his support silently in the stands. He had also come to every game he could when I played in the recreational ball league, JV, and he did the same when I made varsity. I was grateful to have him there even though he would talk my ear off and give me hell on the ride home. Hearing him talk off the wall was a small price to pay to have someone show positive interest in you as a young man.

In the beginning I rarely got off the bench. During the ride home from the first few varsity games, I would sit in silent frustration and stare out the front window. As I stared out the window on the ride home Timmy V would break down how incompetent my coach was. He broke down how the coach mismanaged talent and basically didn't know what he was doing. Timmy V had spent some time in his youth playing ball over seas. I didn't like it, but I had to respect his opinion.

When Timmy V wasn't bashing the coach he was pushing his other agenda. He wasn't shy with his thoughts on what I should be doing with my life and how I could make it better. I would be better off getting a job than wasting time playing under that unqualified coach was part of the usual spiel. The coach wasn't one of my favorite people, but he was only a minor obstacle. I had bigger goals.

Leonard, the athletic freak who lived across street, got a ride home from most practices and games from my parents. I was more than happy when he was in the car with me and Timmy V on the rides home. That meant he got to split the experience of listening to Timmy V hate on everything. Timmy V had made hating an art form.

"Nigga, that coach ain't shit. What you need to do is this," he'd say. "Chasing that ball for them white folks ain't shit. Look at what chasing that ball got your uncle. Nigga, what you need to do is . . ." is all he said day in and day out. The hating drove me crazy, but Leonard loved it. He would be in the back seat rolling with laughter even when he became the subject of the hate.

It was the end of my sophomore year when the head JV coach took a head coaching job at another school. He had nurtured my skill and built up my confidence. Coach Larkin had an open-door policy and if there was something I didn't understand or if I had questions about his tactics, I could walk up to him and ask. You might not like what you heard, but he wouldn't leave you confused about his methods. When he left he took with him the only sounding board I had for basketball.

The prior year on JV I didn't understand why I wasn't playing as much as I thought I deserved. I wanted to know why guys that I was clearly better than were playing ahead of me. When I finally gathered the courage to speak with him one on one he was very straight forward with me.

He said, "Your game is completely street ball; it doesn't translate to how I want to run my team. You over-handle the ball, and you're too flashy. If you continue to work hard and get better things, will work out."

Coach Larkin gave it to me straight. I worked my butt off on trying to improve the problem areas of my game and played all-out on defense in practice and games. As I improved, he started giving me more and more time off the bench. It fueled me to work harder. After a few games he called me in his office and told me I would start the next game.

"You play all-out defense and have become the best defender on the team. You worked hard and improved on the areas that I pointed out. You've earned the right to start."

The varsity coach was a different animal. I worked as hard as I knew how for this man during practice, and he still couldn't manage to learn my name. He only called me by my number, and if he got excited, he called me Fernando. I wasn't discouraged, just confused. It made me work harder. I wanted to earn his respect. During practices I became more and more aggressive. Since I wasn't playing much in the real games, the practices became the real games for me. I approached practice like there was a stand full of people watching me.

One Saturday practice we were having an inter-squad scrimmage, and I caught fire. Coach never put me in with the first team even though I would continuously eat the starting point guard up. I thought if I crushed him every time we went head-to-head that would be the quickest way into the lineup. This particular practice I was trying to make a point, and there would be no way the coach could ignore me anymore. After the first quarter of the scrimmage, I had 10 points and three assists. The rest of the second team and I were up on the scoreboard versus the starting five.

My performance in the first quarter sent my confidence through the roof. The head coach was coaching the starting five, and the ninth grade coach and assistant varsity coach were coaching the second unit. The leash was finally taken off me, and I had a legit chance to display some of my potential. The coach for 9th grade had turned me loose and let me play my game. He was more aware of my skill set because he had taken time to work with me before varsity practice on a few occasions.

Playing opposite the starting five was right up my alley. I always did better playing the underdog. Underdogs aren't expected to put up much of a challenge and nobody expects much out of you. When nobody expects you to win, you're presented with the opportunity to play with reckless abandon. There's nothing to loose. And reckless abandon was my specialty.

After my display in the first quarter, the coach switched me from the 2nd unit over to the 1st. I guessed he wanted to see what I could do running point with the 1st unit. The catch was I was very familiar with most of the people on the 2nd unit. We had a trust for each other. The 2nd unit played JV, three-on-three tournaments, and we had spent two years playing together at summer camps.

When Coach switched me over to the 1st unit it was almost like playing with strangers. I wasn't as comfortable playing with them like I was playing with the 2nd unit. My game was running and gunning, but the first team ran a controlled offense. Every chance I got I wanted to push the ball or create off the dribble. My style of play didn't mesh well with the 1st unit.

The 1st team ran the offense through our star forward, Mark. He was a beast. He had a smooth, left-handed jumper, point guard handles, and a super quick first step. The icing on the cake was he was 6'7". Most of the offense on the 1st team was generated by him off the high left post and that's the way he like it.

Once again Coach didn't speak to me or give me any instruction. He just threw me in there without guidance. I wasn't sure what he wanted out of me so I took a wild guess. I figured the coach had placed me on the 1st team to continue playing my game with them. I didn't think he threw me in there to see if I could stay out of the way. I attempted to run and gun the same way with them as I had with my. Things didn't work out well.

My performance in the second quarter was mediocre to say the least. The first six times I brought the ball up on offense I would pass it off to a wing coming off a curl, or I'd get the ball to the star forward, Mark, in the high post. After the initial pass, I wouldn't touch it again until I was bringing it back up the court during the next possession. I hadn't earned his respect or trust yet so he didn't even bother looking my way. It took a few possessions, but I figured out if I was going to get any offensive opportunities, I was going to have to create them myself.

After grabbing a defensive rebound off a long jumper, I took off up the court. The superstar was going full tilt filling the wing on the left, and the other wing was doing the same on the right. We had a three-on-one. As I closed in to our basket I stopped at the free throw line on a dime. I faked a bounce pass to the superstar on the left, and the defense went with the pass. I then pulled up and took the short jumper from the free throw line. I didn't get my feet set and the shot rimmed out to the right. The guy filling the wing on the right grabbed the rebound and went back up for an easy layup.

I knew fundamental basketball, and I was aware I had made the wrong play, but I had done it purposely. If I was on the 2nd team I would have made the fundamental play. I would have faked the jumper to draw the defense towards me and then hit the 6'7" forward with a bounce pass for a high-percentage shot. I felt he had frozen me out for half a quarter, and I was going to return the favor.

A couple possessions later I brought the ball up on the left and the star forward had his man behind him. He had excellent position for an easy entry pass. I ignored him and did a quick left-to-right crossover at the three point line and got a step on my defender. As I made my drive to The Lane, the look I saw on the superstar's face said it all, "mother fucker!" There was no shot blocker on the second team so I got to the rim and through up a circus layup with my left hand. The ball spun around the rim twice and then dropped in.

I made the bucket, but I should have given the ball up to the forward in the post. I wasn't going to bow down in what I felt was a test of testicles. He was the most talented guy in the region by far, but if he wasn't going to pass to me, I wasn't going to pass to him. This wasn't about basketball for me. It was about respect.

After a few more possessions the horn went off to signal halftime. Things weren't going smoothly, and I needed more than a quarter to figure out how to blend with the 1st team. Both teams headed back to the locker room. Playing with the 1st team was starting off well. I sat in silence on the bench in front of my locker.

As I sat looking down at my feet replaying the first half and gathering my thoughts the shadow of a giant engulfed me. I looked up and made eye contact with the 6'7" giant. His face was not friendly by any means.

He reached down and pushed me against a locker by my neck and said, "PASS ME THE FUCKING BALL!!"

I slapped his hands off me and his hand went right back to my neck. I grabbed a broom to even up the odds, but before we got it cracking for real, a couple of our team mates stepped in and calmed the situation.

That wasn't our first run-in. I had been into it with the superstar and his best friend on the team a couple times in summer camp at ga Southern University. The older players knew I didn't bend to intimidation. They would purposely lure me into wars of words to lure me into wrestling and slap boxing matches. The wrestling matches would usually end with me body slammed and held down while three or four older players beat on me. A little hazing from older guys was a rite of passage and was all in fun. Plus it let them know I was tough enough to take the pseudo beatings.

The situation with the superstar putting his hands on my neck wasn't hazing, that was beef. The situation didn't escalate because cooler heads prevailed. I never gave another thought to beefing with the frustrated superstar. I had bigger problems. He had scholarship offers from everywhere, and his ticket was punched. My concern was that I needed to make the most every opportunity. Coach still didn't bother to give me any guidance so going into the second half, I wasn't sure of how to approach playing with the 1st team. After halftime, I decided to just blend in and tune down my game. I wasn't very effective but after a few possessions, the superstar threw me a bone and fed me a pass for a long three that I clanked off the rim. I had lost my spark for that day and spent the rest of the scrimmage on the 1st team as a third or fourth option.

We had a few more practices but the next game was only a few days later. The next game was against Savannah High. The game Coach informed me I would be starting on the bus ride over. Before the moment he informed me I would be starting I had never felt any pressure or any fear with basketball. Previously, I only had two concerns. How many minutes I would play and how many points I could score off the bench. I had never played more than 10 minutes in a varsity game, but I took pride in never being held scoreless if I got on the court. If I got in the game for four minutes, I made it my business to figure out a way to accumulate four points. The point total was important to me. If you scored, no matter how few points, your named would be on the stat sheet in the paper. My mother didn't come to any of my games, but she clipped the articles from the paper and saved them. Growing up, I saw my uncle with his face on the cover of newspapers and his name all over the place. Having my name on the stat sheet gave me a little taste of that.

Sometimes you pray and ask God for things you think you want. When God blesses you with exactly what you prayed for you may find that you aren't prepared for the blessing. I was physically prepared to start and play, but I wasn't mentally ready. I had spent all my time physically preparing. When I got the news of starting it sent a chill down my body that froze me. I felt my muscles tighten, and I couldn't get loose.

Time sped up and I couldn't get loose or shake my butterflies. Before I knew it, we were tipping the ball. We lost the tip and started out on defense, and they pushed the ball right at us. The 2 guard brought the ball up and passed to the 3, curling off the wing and draining a long jumper. One of our bigs took the ball out the net and passed it off to me. My job was to bring the ball up the court and get us into our first offensive set. To my surprise, the coach from Savannah High had a man-to-man, full-court press on.

A man-to-man, full-court press should have been nothing for me. I could break a full-court press single handedly. My ball handling was my strongest weapon. I could control the ball equally well with both hands and my arsenal of moves was limited only by my imagination. Today was different. I was having an out-of-body experience. I took the inbound pass and pushed the ball against the pressure defense and I went to cross over a defender and wasn't crisp. I was way too high in my stance. I crossed from left to right too slowly, and my opponent jumped my move. I had never gotten the ball stripped from me in a game before, but I got picked clean that time. Before I could turn around to give chase he was laying it up. Pure embarrassment.

My muscles tightened up even more. The forward took the ball out of the net again and passed it to me. Again with the man-to-man, full-court press. I was surprised that I had been picked off, but it was a fluke. It wouldn't happen again. As I was bringing the ball up, I went to make a move and the same guy who had picked me off was there again. This time I crossed him up cleanly. As I made my move, he reached right through my body and slapped my wrist down and caused me to lose the ball. The first time he picked my pockets clean, but the second time it was a blatant foul. To my surprise I didn't hear a whistle. Again, he raced down court for an easy layup.

The ref had let him go straight through me. Eye for an eye. I took matters into my own hands and ran the ball thief down. As he was going up for the layup I gave him a hard foul. He had embarrassed me with the second pick, and I reacted the only way I knew how. My opponent hit both free throws. For the third time, I found myself bringing the ball up court. I hadn't made it past half court and we were already down six points. I had been picked off twice in a row, and I knew the ball thief would be coming in for a third try.

I dribbled up court and waited for the trap to come and it came. Instead of playing good defense they went right for the steal. I waited for him to reach and then I crossed over from right to left and then took the ball behind my back with my left hand back to my right. I had practiced that move since I was a kid and had it down to perfection. When I went behind my back with my left hand, I left both defenders standing there frozen and I was off to the races. His gamble created a semi fast break. I was coming down court full speed; we had a five-on-three situation. I got to the free throw line before they decided to stop the ball. The man guarding our star forward converged on me to stop me from getting all the way to the hoop. I made the easy pass to our star forward on the left baseline, and he finished the easy layup. We were on the board.

After a missed jumper on the other end I received an outlet pass and again was headed down court full tilt.

Nobody bothered to stop the ball, so I kept my dribble and went in for an easy layup. I felt my muscles loosen up and I was ready to play.

On defense I could see the point guard who had picked me twice had a shaky handle. I played off him and baited him to get careless with his dribble. I waited patiently as he pounded the ball into the court using only his right hand. He slowly brought the ball up court. As he crossed half court he took a look back at his coach to get a play. That was my opportunity. I took off and timed my explosion with the moment he turned his head.

Got him back! I picked him clean the same way he had picked me off. I was two steps past him with the ball before he knew what had happened. I was making a race for the rim when I heard a whistle blow.

I thought to myself, "Bullshit!" It was unreal. I had stolen the ball flawlessly and still got hit with the whistle. The reaching foul was my second foul, and I was replaced in the lineup.

I was just getting a rhythm before I was quickly put back in familiar territory: the bench. One advantage of sitting on the bench was I had an opportunity to watch and analyze and let my nerves calm. After sitting on the bench for what seemed like an eternity I could feel my anxiety had completely gone away. When Coach put me back in the game I would crank my intensity up to high power. No more letting nerves make me stink up the joint. I sat on the bench the rest of the first quarter and then to my surprise I sat on the bench the rest of the first half.

At halftime we all sat in the locker while the coach gave another uninspiring half time speech. He rambled on and on but didn't make any point of note or any legitimate halftime adjustments. At the beginning of the third quarter I was for sure I was going back in with the starters but coach left me on the bench. He put back in the old starting point guard.

The time in third quarter ticked away. Still I sat and watched glued to the bench. It was my fault. I had frozen up when Coach sprung that I would be starting on me, but I had snapped out of the brief trance. I was ready to be the aggressor I was during practice and summer camp. The third quarter came to a close. I finished it in the same place where I began it, on the bench.

The fourth quarter began the same as the second and third quarter: with me watching the action from the bench. Internally, I was on the verge of a pity party, but I had only myself to blame. Opportunity had knocked, and I wasn't mentally ready to answer the door. I had put all those hours in getting physically prepared but had choked when my time came. I was disgusted with myself for blowing such a huge opportunity, but I had learned a lesson. If and when I set foot on the court again I would go all out.

With less than two minutes in the game the score was out of reach in the opposing team's favor. The opposing coach cleared his bench. Following the opposition's lead, Coach cleared our bench as well. Finally he put me back in the game. I wasn't in the game 30 seconds before I took my man off the dribble and got an easy bucket. I played defense like it was the fourth quarter of a championship game for those last few seconds. I picked off a lazy pass and raced down court for another easy layup. The plays were good, but it was all during garbage time. Shortly after that the final horn blew.

After the game, Coach gave a short, post-game speech and the practice schedule for the next week. He also spoke on the big game coming up. After everything calmed down I got within speaking distance of Coach to see if he would throw me bone. Again, he walked pass me like I wasn't there. I was expecting him to give me a breakdown of where I could improve or some words of encouragement. The words never came. Once again I felt lost.

On the ride home I felt horrible about how the game had started but I finished strong. After logging less than eight minutes of actual floor time I had six points, one assist, one steal, and two turnovers. The numbers weren't great, but I had made an impact and would get my name in the paper. The next week of practice flew by. I was as aggressive as I ever was and worked my ass off in practice. I needed another chance at starting. I would prove to coach I was ready to run his team. The next game would be the biggest game of the year. That game would give me the greatest stage I had ever played on. It was a chance to redeem and prove myself in front of the entire city.

The week before the game seemed to fly by. I didn't just physically prepare for the game; I mentally prepared for the game. My junior high school football coach in Texas used to make us sit in silence before a game and visualize our playbooks, and visualize ourselves making moves on the field. It never dawned on me to do that with basketball, but after my horrible first two possessions the previous game I implemented the meditating formula into my preparations.

The game was played on a weekend and a lot of my family just happened to be down from Atlanta. I invited everybody out to watch. I was confident. I was going to have my coming out party in front of the entire city and my family. After the Bradwell vs. Liberty game my name would become household terminology in Hinesville. Every day that week I woke up two hours earlier than normal and walked to a court near my house and got two hours of jump shots in before class. I figured everybody else I would be competing with was still sleep. If I was practicing while they were sleeping that meant I would have an edge.

On game day as expected, the gym was packed well beyond capacity. The crowd was standing room only and the atmosphere was electric. I had blown my opportunity to start the game before, but I planned on making amends for my choke session. If I was the coach I would have been reluctant to start me right after that game as well. I was at peace with coming off the bench.

Before the game we lined up in the tunnel outside of our locker room and prepared to run out and start a layup drill. The game was on our home court, so Bradwell was already out shooting layups on one half of the court. For the layup drill, we lined up shortest to tallest. I was the shortest on the team, so I would always get to run out first with the ball and start the drill. I stood waiting at the front of the tunnel listening to the crowd. It was the biggest, most intense crowd I had ever seen. I didn't let them shake me. There was no way I would have a replay of last game.

I had never prepared for anything like I prepared for that game. The knowledge of how much I had prepared gave me a sense of calmness. I was ready.

The sound system in our gym was state-of-the-art and brand new like everything else in the school. Liberty County High had only been in existence for four years, so everything was still new. When the speakers came on the crowd went silent for a brief moment. All you could hear was the beginning of our intro song.

"Boomdun, ont, dun, dun. Thump, thump! Boomdun, ont, dun, dun. Thump! Thump!" The crowd went crazy, and I took off with the ball and started the layup drill.

"Who's that peeking in my window? Pow! Nobody now." We came out to Goody Mob Cell Therapy. It was the hottest song at the time.

You couldn't hear anything but one thing: The crowds for both teams were singing the words to the song. We started the layup drill. You could feel the electricity in the air. The gym was packed with what seemed liked the entire city. I had about 10 family members sitting in the crowd to go along with the hundreds of other people. Up until that point, Timmy V had been my only family member who had seen me play in a live game.

After tipoff, I took my place on the bench and focused hard. I concentrated harder than I had ever concentrated on a game in my life. Consciously, I made sure I kept my breathing under control and my head clear. The last thing I wanted was to have a relapse of choking once my number was called.

The game was exciting. It seemed like the lead would change every two or three minutes. The first quarter ended, and there was only a difference of a few points on the score board. The second quarter began. I hadn't got off the bench and neither did many of the other guys sitting on the bench with me. Normally I would go in with two or three minutes left at the end of the first quarter, but it didn't happen. The score was close, and Coach hadn't subbed much. Coach could only use that seven-man rotation for so long before he wore down the starters. I figured Coach would give the starters a break sometime during the second quarter and I would have my chance. It didn't happen.

There was hardly any talk in the locker room at halftime. We all knew what was at stake. We were up against the cross-town rivals, and this game was our city championship. The third quarter began, and the lead still went back-and-fourth. Our star forward was carrying us, but Bradwell had a beast as well. His name was Will, and he was a freakish athlete who could nearly jump out of the gym. Every time he got loose on a wing during a fast break everybody in the gym held their breath. Everyone knew he would put on a show with his leaping ability.

After the third quarter came to a close the game was still close. Coach had almost exclusively played the starters. He did shuttle in a different wing and big men for a few seconds, but he kept our star forward and our point guard in without a breather for most of the game. The game clock was ticking away, and I was starting to get nervous. It was the fourth quarter, and I still hadn't touched the floor. I had always gotten at least four or five minutes by the half, and that's all I would have needed. The fourth quarter quickly started to wind down. Bradwell made a run and took a commanding lead. Our starters were tired and had broken down at the end. Our rivals didn't take mercy and continued to build a cushion. When I looked up at the clock, there was less than two minutes left.

The crowd had settled down, and a lot of people had cleared the gym. There still were a lot of people in there, but it was no longer a packed house. That was when I heard the worse sound I had ever heard.

"Put in number 3! Put in number 3! Put in number 3!" My family had started a chant and was getting louder and louder.

"No! No! No!" I said to myself. Anything but that. They meant well, but the last thing I wanted was attention drawn to me while I sitting on the bench feeling helpless. As they chanted, I felt my eyes welling up. I didn't know what to do with all this emotion. I felt disappointed, and now they were adding in embarrassment. I didn't let a tear fall, but if someone would have gently tapped me it probably would have caused one to fall.

Again I heard the chants, "Put in number 3! Put in number 3! Put in number 3!"

I looked up at the clock and it showed one minute left, and that's when the coach looked down his bench at me and three or four other people who hadn't played. He signaled for us to enter the game. I knelt down at the scorers' table and looked back up at the clock showing 45 seconds and counting down. Luckily for us, a foul was committed so we got in. After the free throws, a forward inbounded the ball to me and I raced up the court and passed off to the 2 guard on the wing after bringing the ball past half court. I cut straight through The Lane and came off a pick and flared out toward the three point line. As I came out my curl I made eye contact with the 2 guard and he sent me a pass.

There was no way I was going to miss this three. My pride was riding on one shot. As the pass came my way, my eyes enlarged at what I was seeing. The pass came flying in wildly and was so low it hit me in the back of my ankle. I tried to get low enough to save it but it was no use. I couldn't. The ball rolled out of bounds. Change of possession. Bradwell took the ball out and dribbled out the rest of the clock. I was devastated. I had gotten myself up so high for the challenge to have everything still go terribly wrong. I had no control over how much playing time I was given. I felt humiliated in front of my family. I had bragged so much before the game because I was confident I would play and play well. Worse than the embarrassment, I felt cheated out of the second opportunity to redeem myself.

I don't remember hearing a single word from the coach's post-game talk. I was having a breakdown. I had pumped myself up so high and told everybody that would listen that I was going to break out at home in front of everybody. I contemplated sitting in the locker room and waiting for the crowd to clear, but I decided to walk out and face my people. Walking out that locker room to face all my family and friends took the last little bit of mental strength I had left. I felt like I was naked and exposed. I wasn't D-Ray. I could feel my family from Atlanta looking at me like I was a fraud. They had heard I could play, but all they saw me do was fumble a ball off my leg out of bounds.

My family had taken three cars to the game, and two were already packed. The only car I could ride in was with Timmy V. He had driven up to the game alone. I was hurting. I felt weak and vulnerable. As soon as I sat in the car with him he started in. It was the same speech he had continuously given me for two years straight.

"You're running behind that ball like a fool. You know what I would do if I were you? I would quit that team! If I were you, I would get a job and start saving up to get a car. That coach ain't shit, and y'all lost because of him. What the hell he got a bench for if he's not going to use it? I'm telling you to look at your uncle D-Ray. What did running behind that ball for those white folks get him?"

In my weakened state I could feel my mind grow empty. His words entered my ear and filled my soul, my heart, and my mind. Everything around me turned gray. I went numb and lost my will to fight his advice. His words vibrated in my head. For the first time he had gotten past my defense. What he said finally made sense to me. If a world-class athlete like D-Ray had failed to sustain his dream in the NFL what was the point in working so hard to accomplish my dreams? That night I quit playing basketball. I was infected.

# GLADIATOR SCHOOL

I didn't have any aspirations to live in Liberty, Texas anymore, but going back home always thrilled me. I loved being back at home for the summer months, and this would be my last summer as a child. The following summer I'd be finished with high school and officially a man in the eyes of the world. I could unplug and relax when back home in the country. The pressures of my life in Georgia didn't exist at home. In Liberty, everybody walked like me, talked like me, and thought like me. In Texas I didn't feel like an alien. When I was home, I felt like I didn't have to second guess people's true intentions or wonder about whom I could or who I couldn't trust.

When I left Georgia, I left my problems there and I wouldn't give them another thought until I returned. My issues in Georgia didn't exist in Texas, and my issues in Texas didn't exist in Georgia. It was like living in two different worlds. I was almost a different person in each of my worlds. My ethics and principles never changed, but the things that tested my ethics and principles changed when I swapped states. In Georgia I had no family besides my brother. In Texas everybody, everything, and everywhere had something to do with my family.

My mind was consumed with college, basketball, friends, foes, jobs, high school, and peer pressure when I was in Georgia. There were so many problems that came with being in the stage that comes between childhood and adulthood. It's extremely confusing trying to find a place to fit in society without a blueprint or roadmap. Texas was the remedy for all that ailed me in Georgia. In Texas I was a man, and people treated me as such. People gave me space and didn't second guess me. There was little adult instruction and so much freedom; I loved it. There would be no micromanagement from Timmy V or my mother for two months.

Liberty was home. It felt good to be back on the same streets where I started. It had been over a year and half since I had been home, but things hadn't changed much from the look of things. There weren't any new houses, people, or businesses. Things looked as if they had been frozen in time from the last time I was home.

The name of the neighborhood my family occupied was Wallisville Road, better known as The Lane. It was a strip of road half of a mile long that branched off of 563 Farm Road. Most of my immediate family lived off 563, but the largest concentration was on The Lane. My maternal and paternal grandmothers both lived on The Lane. My dad, four or five of his brothers, and his only sister lived there. Two of my mother's brothers and their families also lived on The Lane. To say I was kin to everybody was an understatement. Besides all my legitimate uncles and aunts, my maternal grandfather had countless illegitimate kids. At least five or six of my illegitimate uncles and aunts lived within a mile of The Lane. My brother and I could trace some kind of blood tie to everybody in every house on The Lane.

Growing up around so much family didn't mean you didn't have problems with people. It meant exactly the opposite. There was always tension. Family could hate, love, or envy you better than anybody else in the world could. The difference with family and everybody else was your family could go up side your head with a brick, but by nightfall you would be playing video games. Beefs with family could never erase the fact that you were blood. That was the strongest bond I knew of.

We constantly beefed amongst ourselves, but when we stepped off The Lane into the rest of Liberty, we unified. Everybody everywhere knew how deep we were and that we would swarm on any hood as a whole if there was any beef. The irony of that cloak of invincibility was that we gained most of our reputation cutting our teeth on each other. As just as vicious as we were when we cliqued up, we were twice that amongst ourselves. The Lane was a gladiator school pumping out country thugs.

The main cast of characters I grew up with was composed of five relatives of similar age to me. Big H, GB, Booby-trap, Youngsta, and Gene, were the main group of guys I had interacted with. We were all brothers or first cousins with the exception of Youngsta. Youngsta was as close to kin to us as possible without having blood ties.

Youngsta lived across the street, and we maintained a hate-tolerate type of relationship. More than half of the confrontations I had experienced up to that point had been with him directly. Youngsta was the only other light skinned boy my age I knew. Our skin complexion was where the comparisons stopped. He wasn't pretty, harmless looking, or respectable like people described me. When people spoke about him, they usually said something about how bad he was. Before he was a teenager, he had the look of somebody that had been to prison and was ready to go back. His face had scratches and scars of no known origin for as long as I could remember. Those marks gave him a hardened look. He possessed a very questionable character unless it was 563 versus them. He was always all in like the rest of us, and I would fight to death for him in the streets. I knew for a fact he would do the same for me.

The thing that linked Youngsta and me and kept us at each other's throats was our eternal struggle for dominance over the other. We both longed to be the alpha male, and we both wanted to be known as the hardest lil' nigga on our street. Neither one of us ever wanted to bow down or let the other gain the alpha position.

Things came to a head a between us a few years prior to the summer of '96. I was spending time in Texas enjoying another carefree summer of no work and no school. At that age, my most prized possession was still my bike. My bike was my symbol of freedom. It allowed me to get to places faster and farther than I would have been able to reach walking.

One of my favorite destinations was about half a mile up 563 and located behind Turkey Creek Baptist Church. Turkey Creek was the church of my family, but that's not where I was headed. I was riding my bike to Turkey Creek because my uncle gadget lived behind the church. I love riding down to my uncle's house. He would always have some food smoking on the grill, cold sodas, and he would slide me a beer if I wanted one. My uncle gadget was also a comedian. He would constantly tell me adult jokes and have me cracking up laughing. Beyond the superficial benefits of hanging with gadget was the real reason I hung out with him: He gave me an outlet to speak freely to an adult man and get unbiased information about life.

One hot Texas morning I walked out of my Grandma Ellen's house with plans of riding my bike down to gadget's house. I picked my bike up from the ground in her yard exactly where I had left it. We were in the country. It was safe to leave your belongings lying around anywhere on the block and expect it to be there when you got back. If my bike happened to not be where I left it, it didn't mean that it was stolen. That meant somebody had borrowed it and left it somewhere. It would piss me off if somebody rode my bike up the street and left it, but it wasn't the end of the world.

I picked my bike off the ground and I didn't notice anything that would raise a flag at first. I did notice a couple of my cousins watching me out the side of their eyes while they sat on the porch. It was like they were waiting for something to happen.

When I twisted the handlebars on my bike something felt terribly wrong. There was no fluid motion, something was different.

"Am I tripping?" I asked myself. When I gave the handlebars another twist I could hear the metal grind on metal. "What the fuck is wrong with my bike?"

I looked at my cousins and they looked toward Youngsta who was across the street. He had two or three bike frames torn apart at his feet. He was taking some pieces off one and putting them on another and so forth.

"That nigga took the ball bearings out of your bike," one of my cousins replied in a jokey joke way. I wasn't laughing. There wasn't anything funny about the situation from my perspective. There I was ready to ride my bike to my uncle's house and I couldn't make a move because this fool has stolen my damn ball bearings. I carefully thought about my next move.

I didn't feel like fighting or want any drama. I just wanted my bike restored to its original form. I grabbed my bike and I walked it across the street and laid it in front of Youngsta. Politely but firmly I engaged him.

"Say, cuz. Fix my bike like it was." I didn't ask him any questions so he didn't have a chance to lie or get buck with me. He didn't say anything and took the bike and moved it in front of where he was sitting. I took that as his acknowledgement that he had wronged me and he was going to set things straight. I went back across the street and sat on the porch and waited for him to repair my bike.

As I sat on the porch my eyes stayed glued to him like a hawk. To my surprise he went right to work on my bike and brought it back over to me within a few minutes. I was in shock. This nigga actually tried to do the honorable thing and repair my bike. Everything would be cool and we both would live to battle another day.

I took my bike from his possession and I gave the handlebars a turn. I heard the same sound I had heard before—the sound of metal on metal. My anger was starting to build.

"Say bruh, my bike ain't right. Man you messed up my bike and you need to fix it back like it was."

He snatched the bike out my hands and headed back to his yard to give it another go. I headed back to the porch and my cousins were entertained as they watched.

He again broke the bike down as I watched from the porch. After watching on the porch with my cousins for a few minutes, I became restless. I started becoming angry thinking about all the time Youngsta had wasted of mine stealing parts off my bike. I walked to the side of my grandmother's house. There was a little section where one of my uncles worked on lawn mowers. In his makeshift workstation there were a couple lawn mowers broken down, small parts and tools lying about. I looked around and daydreamed about learning to work on motors one day when someone had time to teach me. The day dream was broken by the sound of Youngsta walking my bike into the yard. He brought the bike up to me and had a real salty look on his face like he was losing patience from doing me a favor. I didn't like his lack of humbleness but I wasn't in the mood for a fight. I just wanted my bike repaired so I could get on with my business.

I took the bike from him and gave the handle bar a quick twist back and forth. Same damn noise. "Say, this shit ain't fixed!" "Take this bike and fix it!"

Both of us had run out of patience. At that moment we locked eyes, and we both knew what it was going to be.

"Nigga I ain't fixing shit, fuck you and that bike."

He might as well have spit in my face instead of his next move. He turned his back and started to walk off like he was dealing with a bitch. Now this was the nigga I knew.

All honor was gone from the situation. We had been in plenty of fist fights about petty disagreements but I had never stolen from him and he had never stolen from me. He had crossed a line into new territory. He had violated my property in our hood where everything was supposed to be safe.

In my mind I had just been pissed on. He had stole out my yard and then added insult to it by cussing me out and then turning his back on me. My heart pumped like it was going to jump out my chest. Something had to be done. I couldn't see my cousins around the corner on the porch but I knew they had saw and heard everything. My reputation is what protected me, and it's what got me respect. This nigga had just disrespected me with people watching.

Did this nigga really just turn his back on me and walk off? Did he think that would be the end? We had been through this ritual to many times for him to think I would let him get away with that. My mind blanked from anger and I reached down and grabbed the first thing I put my hand on. It probably was one of the worst things I could have put my hands on. It was a hammer.

I ran up behind him and before he had a chance to turn around and defend himself. I swung at the hammer like I meant it. It landed right in the middle of his back making a loud thud as it made contact. His back arched forward from the pain and in an attempt to dodge the next blow. There would be no dodging.

It felt like I left and something else took over my body. I lost all control over myself and became an animal. He tried to strike out running but I was on him to close. I tackled him and pinned him down with his face in the ground and then I started to beat on his back. The hammer hitting his flesh made no noise in my mind after the first hit. I couldn't hear him screaming or crying out. There was nothing but complete silence as I worked. I don't know how many times I struck him but one time was too many. The only thing that broke me out of my daze and stopped me from striking him again and again was my cousins running toward me screaming. They stared at me in disbelief.

I stood up in and was also in shock at what I was cable of doing. The hammer still in my grip felt evil. I wanted it gone so I threw it as hard as I could. It landed somewhere in the woods in the back of my grandmother's house. When I turned around Youngsta was standing up. We were facing off again. How could he be standing and ready to square off with me after what I had just done to him? Why wasn't he being carried off by cousins back to his home? This nigga was a warrior.

My toughness was something I took pride in. I wasn't the biggest, fastest, quickest, or baddest person, but I was toughest. I never backed down, I never ran, and I would never accept a defeat. When Youngsta stood up and faced me after what I had did to him I knew had met at the very least my equal. For a moment I felt a fear come over me. Youngsta had taken the best that I could dish out and came back ready for more.

As we stood facing off we had a brief moment of our eyes locking and then he charged in with his head down. He bull rushed in and tried to tackle me same as he always did. We had been in so many fights I knew his style better than he did. I won majority of my conflicts with Youngsta because he was predictable. All I had to do was wait until he charged me. I would take a step back to throw off his charge and then unload with hooks and upper cuts. This time I would do things differently. He had taken my best, stood threw it and came back for more. If he could take me beating him with a hammer, I could stand in there and take his bullrush.

He rushed in and I stood my ground. Not one step back. He collided with me and drove his shoulder into my abdomen. The force he tackled me with almost caused me to flip over his back but he locked his arms around my waist and took me to the ground with a thud. After we hit the ground we jostled and rolled around both trying to gain a dominant position. We rolled back and forth and exchanged a couple of punches before my cousins stepped in and broke us up. I was so high on adrenalin that I don't remember who the two cousins were that intervened.

In a traditional setting the community would have outcast me for attacking another person with a hammer. The 563 wasn't traditional community. Boys were encouraged to behave in the way me and Youngsta behaved. If you had a problem with somebody talking it was feminine. Problems were resolved by getting physical. Those were the rules.

I wasn't disciplined or counseled for my action by anyone. No adult said a single word to me about what I had did. Instead of punishment I received the opposite. I was celebrated. My actions gained me more respect and added to my reputation. No parents stopped sending their kids out to interact with me. The only difference was that it confirmed what people probably already thought about me.

I had no second thoughts on what I had done. There was no harm so there was no foul. Youngsta was back on the block the next day. It was business as usual until I received a wakeup call. The eye opening revelation was instigated by Khandi. Khandi was Younsta's female cousin who lived in the same house with him.

A few days after the incident, I was on the block going about my business of hanging out as usual. The situation was over and I had moved on. Khandi walked right up to me while I was laughing and having a good time and unleashed her perception of me.

"You know what Te'? You a fuck nigga. What you did was fucked up!"

All I could do was sit there and listen to her speak from the heart.

"You sit here like it is all good, but you don't know what you did to my cousin. I had to sit there all night and listen to him crying out while my grandma tended to the bruises you put on his back."

I didn't respond. There was nothing to say to her. The after effect of my actions on other people never crossed my mind. That night after Khandi broke me down I dreamed the tables were turned on me. It was me who had been beaten with the hammer, and it was me with the bruised back. My conscious started to eat away at me and it still does. I stopped interacting with people for a while. I just wanted to be alone.

Around this same time I was also trying to deal with my mother being deployed to Iraq for the first gulf war.

There was too much going on in my head for my young mind to grasp. A couple members of my family caught on to my strange behavior and sent me to Arkansas for a month to get my head straight.

After returning from Arkansas I felt calmer, but my conscious still weighed heavy on me. I could never get comfortable around Youngsta again. I knew one day it might be me on the other end of the hammer.

Youngsta wasn't around for the summer of '96. He was locked up that summer, but everybody else was on deck. Booby Trap and my brother ran supper tight as they always had. During the summer if you saw one you saw the other. They rarely separated. They looked alike and walked a like. If you didn't know them personally most likely you wouldn't have been able to identify one from the other. My brother Gene was a little slimmer and taller than the shorter and thicker Booby. They were two of the slickest out everyone. You never caught them with their hands dirty or around any trouble when they were young but that was all for show. As we all got older I learned those two were the wildest they just kept their business amongst themselves.

GB and Big H were the other two boys my age on the block. They were brothers. GB was very similar to me in some of his mannerism. He was more laid back then me and had an even temper but would snap. GB was also very calculating with his moves. He would sit back and watch situations on fold and soak up the game even when you didn't think he was watching. He was smart enough were he could turn the tables over on you without you ever knowing it was him.

I was a little less than a year older than GB, but he was younger than me so he was my responsibility. I felt the same way about Booby and Gene. I was the oldest and it was my duty to look out for them. When we were younger GB would come and get me if he had a problem with somebody he might not be able to take in a fight. If he brought his beef to me I was obligated to take the fight. If he felt that strongly that I could protect him then I wasn't going to let him down. I relished in the fact that he respected my gangsta' enough to ask for my help with a problem.

GB and I ran tight, but he also spent a lot of time with his cousins on his mom's side as well. Sometimes his hanging with his cousins meant trouble for me. One of his cousins in particular always made me nervous when he was around. We called him Redd. The last fight we had I caught him off guard playing football. I took full advantage of him letting his guard down. That whipping I gave him that day was nothing compared to what he had did to me a few years before. He put a scar on mind I would never forget.

It was too far in the past to remember all the details but Red and I were very small kids at the time and ended up in a small skirmish. Somehow during the fight he pinned me down on the ground and he mashed my face into a pile of ants. He wasn't satisfied with mashing my face in the ants. He took it to the next level and held my face down in the ant bed until somebody pulled him off of me. After that experienced I was never got too scared to lock up with anybody else. What can be worse than being held down while having your face eaten on by fire ants?

If growing up on The Lane off 563 didn't teach me anything it taught me how to be a warrior. We were all gladiators and The Lane was our school.

# MONEY

Running the streets of Liberty with my family was a welcomed change of pace from the slow, dragging school year in Hinesville. When H and I linked up during the summers we both morphed into more aggressive versions of selves. We fed off each other's energy to power up and become bigger than life characters. In hind sight, looking back at the effects we had on each other it was best for both of us that there were 800 miles between us 10 months out of cach year. Our time running the streets together would be short so we would subconsciously squeeze a year worth of adventure into 2 months. We gave the streets hell during the summer.

My life styles contrasted considerably between Texas and Georgia. How I negotiated the streets of Texas and how I maneuvered the sidewalks of Georgia were polar opposite. I was Dr. Jekyll and Mr. Hyde. In Georgia I assumed the role of the quiet run of the mill school boy. Once my feet crossed the Texas borderline and I was back in Liberty I morphed back into the flamboyant, fast talking player I was raised to be.

Personality wise, H and I shared many similarly. Our mannerisms and view of our place in the world were almost identical and there wasn't much we disagreed on. We had been raised by the same people and grew up exploring the same streets. Beyond our blood ties and mannerisms we also gravitated toward the same vices. We both possessed an insatiable craving for adventure, fast money, and fast women. The safety net of our camaraderie gave us the green light to chase our vices with no regard for consequences. As a tandem, we got ourselves into situations that neither of us would have chanced solo.

In our pursuit of adventure and fast women we were identical, but fast money was something we saw from different sides of the fence. My approach to making money was a two part hustle. The first part of the hustle was to generate money. I generated money by cutting yards, washing cars, or doing any small work I could find for chump change. The second part of the hustle was to then try and flip the chump change into longer money. Flipping money in a dice game was the easiest and quickest way I had discovered to turn my chump change into something decent.

My counterpart had different ideas about earning a living. Around the time we were approaching our teenage years H started earning his pocket money running errands for dope boys. The game was a natural fit for H. As we grew the more physically intimidating he became but he maintained his calm demeanor.

We were no older than 12 when H took me to work with him in a trap for the first time. I don't remember too much about it besides sitting around and waiting while H did his thing. The dope house he worked out of was on The River. His main job was to roll up marijuana cigars. The cigars were known by the locals as "sweets." That one day on the job was enough for me. Sitting and watching hour after hour as he H and another teenage girl a little older than us rolled sweet after sweet. That hustle wasn't for me. I couldn't sit still for that long.

By time 1996 rolled around we weren't grown men yet but we were far from being little boys. As we grew bigger the expenses of our player lifestyle grew and got bigger right along with us. Our new habits had to be supported so the years of small money hustling became a thing of the past. It was time to get into grown man money making. 19'96 my understanding about my place in the world drastically changed from what it once had been. I started to see life threw a man's eyes and no longer as a naive child.

The worldlier I became the more I realize how big of a factor money and sex were playing in the dealings of everything that was going on around me. I learned early about the different types of women available to a man. Before I stepped foot off the porch I knew the difference between whores and house wives. The concept of money was different. A lot of important things were made clear to me by watching and observing others, but money wasn't something I could master being a spectator. Money was something I had to learn on my own.

As important as the knowledge of money is to be successful in the adult world I would soon be joining it would seem that someone would have taken the time to attempt to enlighten me. Ironically nobody from my environment spoke or talked on the game of controlling money. On every other corner I turned there was a man willing to talk his face blue on the subjects of manipulating women and being hard and tough in the street. No one ever spoke on the subject of manipulating money or being hard and tough with green-backs. Guess, you can't teach what you don't know.

# COOKIE MONSTER

Eager to start the summer at full throttle I woke at the crack of dawn my second day back on The Lane. I wasn't sleepy and I wasn't ready to begin the day so I just lay in the bed. Laying in the bed I could hear my grandmother, Mazolia, already up and cooking breakfast. It wouldn't take long before The Lane came alive.

As I lay waiting in the bed my bed room door flung open. It was only at about 8 a.m. but that's mid morning in the country.

"What it do nefff—feeuww!" My uncle gadget strolled into my bedroom with a cold beer in each hand. He had greeted me in similar fashion the previous summer. My uncle had created a beer for breakfast ritual between us and from my perspective it showed he acknowledged me as a man. I was only sixteen but he handed me a beer and I took a swig. I hadn't even had a chance to brush my teeth, but the beer was cold, and I was a man. My uncle assumed that I was mature enough to handle my drinking, but if I couldn't handle it he was going to teach me through practice. In Liberty, men drank.

I guzzled the beer as fast as I could then jumped in the shower. After cleaning up I met back up with gadget on the porch and we chopped it up for a few minutes. He quickly brought me up to speed on all the local happenings that

I had missed while living in Georgia. He then proceeded to show me all the new projects he had going on around his house. During the tour he cracked a few jokes and we both drank a second beer. Every year that I returned me and my uncle would drink a beer and catch up first thing in the a.m. I enjoyed the small rituals between me and my uncles. I looked forward to them as much as I looked forward to running the streets with my cousins.

We didn't talk long before H pulled up to my grandmother's yard in his daddy's old Chevy truck. He came to scoop me up early to make sure I didn't start roaming the streets on my own. In the country people didn't wait around until twelve in the afternoon to start coming out the house. People got up and out early and the streets were full by 8:30-9:30 a.m. I broke camp with my uncle and jumped in the truck with H. It was time to get the summer started.

I didn't bother to ask where we were headed. I assumed we were going to link up with some young broads. H always kept a couple girls on deck for us to kick it with when I came home for summer break. Securing a couple of summer flings was usually how we jump started a summer full of adventure. This time I was mistaken. This time was different.

After driving five minutes, we pulled up on The River. The River was another black hood similar to The Lane except it was about five times the size of The Lane. The River was located within walking distance from the Trinity River, and that's where the name came from. The River was a lively place for a young country boy to spend his time. There was a mom and pops store on one corner, some homes moon lighted as beer bootleggers, and others were part time crack houses. There were multiple traps, and there were junkies walking up and down the streets. On The River there was always something to get into.

Another plus of hanging on The River was it full of young girls. Most of the girls there had too much mileage to take them serious but they were plenty to play with. The girls on The River talked fast and came off harder than the boys around there.

On the ride to The River H had mention something about needing to score a cookie. At the moment I wasn't quite sure what a cookie was so I pretended like I was hip to the game he was talking. I knew if I had to ask what a cookie was I would appear like a lame. A cookie was obviously hustle terminology and if I waited it out I would pick up the meaning soon enough. I had been out the hood to long and felt square being ignorant to a term he used so freely.

Soon After we entered The River H pulled the truck up to the front yard of a beat down trailer house. It was located beside an empty lot where Peppers once stood. Peppers use to be a make shift juke joint that looked like a poorly constructed shed. I was too young to have been a patron of Peppers but my link to now gone juke joint was strong.

Every time I saw the cleared lot Peppers once stood my thoughts would flash back 10 years. A thousand memories of the car rides to pick up my maternal grandfather Joe Lewis would stream into my consciousness. We use to pull up to Peppers and always find my grandfather, "Papa Joe," sitting outside on the bench in front of the club. As always, he would be dressed in his old military-issue jacket and in the same condition: drunk as a skunk and mad. My aunts and uncles dreaded the chore of having to go pick up their father. There would always be an argument or fight for the right not to go get him.

"You dirty summa bitch, what took you so long?" "Hurry the fuck up and let me in the car."

That was the normal greeting from my papa gave to his escort home. He was hell to his wife and kids when he was drunk but no matter what his condition he always treated like I was his favorite person in the world. I was his first grandchild.

When I was younger I would always glance toward the bench seat every time someone drove me past Peppers. More times than not my grandfather Jo would be sitting on that bench outside of Peppers getting full. For years seeing him outside of Peppers was a normal occurrence but it didn't last long forever. My grandfather died when I was eight from cirrhosis of the liver.

The trailer we parked in front of was on its last leg. It wouldn't last too many more moons. If I was a home inspector I would have condemned it at first glance and then set it on fire. It was old, worn out, and wasn't close to being level. The wood the porch was constructed out of had seen ten seasons to many. As we navigated to the door I exercised extreme caution stepping across the rotten planks. Falling threw a porch wasn't how I wanted to get my summer started.

I had hung out on the outside of that trailer before but had never ventured in. Why we needed to enter now was beyond me. I wasn't aware of any girls worth dealing with living in that trailer, and if there weren't any girls to be had, then I wasn't interested in spending one minute of my summer hanging around that old-ass trailer. H was like me so I knew he had to have had a good reason for stopping there.

H parked the truck and we made our way up the porch. H knocked a quick pattern on the door and announced himself. After a few seconds the door opened up. Upon entry we were greeted by one of two brothers whom had set up shop in the trailer. The trailer was small so from the door you could see the kitchen, the living room and down the hall toward the bedrooms. The second of the two brothers was in the kitchen seated at a small round table. The way he sat behind that table looking at us was like he was the president and we had just entered his Oval Office.

I had been in and out of Texas so much I constantly had to get reacquainted with people when I was back home. As we ran the streets H reintroduced me to people in the hood he thought I might not remember or might not remember me. He made a conscious effort to make it as comfortable as possible around strange company for me. H was well aware that I wasn't going to sit still long around people I wasn't comfortable with.

H introduced me the same way he always had. "Y'all remember my cousin Monte from Atlanta? Larry, Jean's son."

After an introduction people usually recognized me or pretended they did. Hearing that I was from Atlanta always broke the ice and lead to questions about the black Mecca. The irony was I didn't live in Atlanta, but

Atlanta was all people in Texas knew about Georgia. It had become pointless to keep telling folks I lived 20 miles outside of Savannah. They wouldn't remember and they would go back to referring to my place of residence as Atlanta within the hour. I made it a point to tell people I didn't live in Atlanta, but it didn't matter; Atlanta and Georgia were synonymous.

After my reintroduction, the brother that opened the door said in a matter of fact way, "I know who that nigga is; that's Te'. You that little nigga that like to fight."

I still wasn't sure what we were doing in the trailer so I was watching everybody's every move. The brother that opened the door's demeanor was cool and he smiled a lot when he talked. He talked in a manner that everything he was saying came out like a punch line. I didn't pick up a bad vibe from him but that didn't mean he wasn't a threat to my safety. He was an inch or two taller than I, dark skin, pudgy, and had short bald fade brush-cut.

The other brother was still seated at the kitchen table and had begun rolling up a sweet. Even though he was seated I could easily see he was not a little man by any means. The physical difference in appearance of the brothers reminded me of Danny DeVito and Arnold Schwarzenegger in the movie *Twins*.

H was 17 years of age, but he was physically larger than most grown men. He stood 6'2 and weighed around 220. The brother sitting at the table was of similar height, but looked about 20 pounds heavier than H. He was a physically intimidating figure. I was only 5'7 and 130 pounds on my best day and being in that small room made me feel vulnerable.

After the first glance at the brother seated at the table I knew from the start I was looking at a man with a lot of player in him. His perfectly pressed perm was neatly pulled back into a pitch black shoulder length pony tail. As he and H spoke back and forth I caught a glance at what looked like six 18-carat gold crowns on the top row of teeth with the same on his bottom row.

Everything appeared kosher but I wasn't letting my guard down. I was still watching everything and everyone like a hawk. As we approached the table the big cat sitting behind it put down the sweet he was rolling then stood up to greet us. As he stood I realized this nigga was much bigger than I anticipated. He dapped H, dapped me, sat back down, and went back to rolling the sweet. H took a seat at the table in front of the big cat. I maintained my position and stood a couple feet behind H to let them conduct their business, and kept my back to a wall and my left shoulder pointed towards the door just in case. It hadn't taken me long to realize where I was. There was no getting comfortable in a crack house.

As H and the big cat sat at the table exchanging words, I picked up on the dynamics of their relationship. The age difference between the two was no more than three years, but their roles were clearly defined: The big cat had taken H under his wing and was grooming him.

As they spoke back and forth the catch word "cookie" came up again. I figured it was something to do with dope before we had gotten out of the truck, but the small details I still wasn't sure about. My best option was to keep my face straight and absorb what was going on around me. If they kept talking I would keep learning. After the parameters of the deal were agreed on the big cat called out his brother's name and gave him a signal. His brother got up off the couch and disappeared into a room in the back of the trailer. When he reappeared he handed something off to his brother and then he went and sat back down on the couch. The big cat eyes lit up and he smirked as he glanced down at what he gripped in his palm. After he finished looking over what he had in his hand he sat it down on table, and pushed it toward H.

My eyes locked in on the saran wrapped slab of crack sliding across the table. It was the size of a small chocolate chip cookie. As H examined cookie the big cat leaned his chair back on the hind legs, took out a jewelry rag, and whipped his gold teeth. As he leaned back the big cat grinned and bragged on his crack cooking skills. He was proud and very pleased with himself. He advised H to observe the color, and to check how hard it had locked up. There weren't any crumbs or shake in the plastic bag. There was only the hard yellowish white crack cookie.

After the exchange H and The big cat wrapped up the transaction and brought business to a close. H stood up from the table and had already stashed the work somewhere on his person before I had a chance to take notice.

After business came to a close we dapped the brothers, H and I started to make our way out the trailer. Before we had gotten out the trailer completely me and the big cat spoke briefly.

"Say, Te' let me holla' at you. "You know if there's anything you need while you're down here I got ya. You know where to find me."

I knew what time it was so I gave a brief response and kept it moving. H was his protégé, not me, and I wasn't interested in becoming one of his soldiers or being schooled by him. I looked him in the eyes to show no disrespect and no fear and gave a vanilla reply.

"I'll keep that in mind." I dapped him and made my exit. After I caught back up with H outside the trailer, we decided it was time we went about our business of getting the summer started.

# SITTING AND WATCHING

My cousins and I had been raised in such close quarters from infancy we had all developed a sort of sixth sense for reading each other's mind. We could communicate with out a lot of talk and we had become predictable to one another. After watching the transaction between H and the big cat my adrenaline was pumping and my mind was racing. I had spent most of my youth watching the game from the sidelines. Sitting and watching was getting old. I didn't have to tell H that I was contemplating an entry. He could sense it.

We left the broke down crack house posing as a trailer house, the two hustling brothers and stepped straight into the mix. The old half cleared lot that once had been my grandfathers stumping grounds was still swarming with people but it was something now different. There was no longer a juke standing there. It had been converted into a trap. My new found curiosity had changed my perception of the possibilities of the trap. Before the trap was no more than a hang out spot. Most of my cousins and friends had some type of dealings in the trap. If I wanted to hang out with people then the trap is where I had to be.

I hadn't invested much thought into the potential of the trap but now my eyes were opening up to new facets. My mind had been so one tracked and locked in on becoming a successful athlete the possibility of becoming a business man never crossed my mind. I was no longer pursuing being an athlete so my mind was free to explore other avenues of opportunity.

Did I have what it would take to be a hustler? I wasn't sure but what I did know is I was lost as far as life after basketball and I felt empty. Not having a passion for anything anymore had created a void and I needed something to feel that hole. Maybe the trap could offer what I was looking for.

H and I made our way into the trap and H started setting up his shop. As he went about his business I searched for a spot to post up and be out the way while he did his thing. I wasn't there to do business. I wasn't a trapper yet and I wanted to sit back and consciously watch the game. Bingo! I spotted an old junk car that was out of commission. It was sitting close enough for me to see and hear everything but it far enough so that I wouldn't be in the way. The junk car was the perfect perch for me to sit and watch.

I quickly surveyed as much as I could. Leading to the trap there were three entry/exit points that formed a T. The trap sat at the center of the intersection. You could see any and everything approaching from at least a quarter of a mile in all three directions.

As I observed the trap it morphed into a makeshift marketplace. Goods were being bought, sold, and exchanged around the clock. Trappers played the roles of the self employed merchants but would become consumers occasionally as well. The main business of this trap in particular was the hand to hand peddling of low level drugs. Crack and weed. The drug trade was primary but there were other business transactions taking place constantly. Hustlers of all kind would wonder in and out of the trap and set up shop for short periods of time. Hustlers selling tennis shoes, clothes, and electronics out the trunk of their cars would frequent the intersection. Makeshift home stores located nearby also took advantage of the constant traffic at the intersection. The home stores sold cold drinks, candy, and fried fish and chicken plates.

When H set up shop there were already three or four trappers busy applying their craft. As business was being ran I observed that there seemed to be an adherence to basic business etiquette. Each trapper made a conscious effort to not blatantly step on anyone else's toes. Most of everybody out there was related and that probably played a large part into the calmness of trap. Things didn't seem to be very competitive.

Every trapper conducted his business with his own method of operation. There was no uniformity between the hustlers. Some accepted short payments, cut deals, and gave out their product on credit. On the other side of the fence there was the other type. H was definitely the other type. There wasn't any negotiating or deal brokering. H was quick to offer a crackhead a beating for the mere mention of his product on credit or short money. Crackheads would walk right past one trapper like he was invisible to buy from his preferred supplier. It wasn't because the quality of product because from what I gathered the big cat was the only supplier and cooker of all the "hard," AKA "crack rock," in the trap. The crackheads knew what I was learning. Some trappers cut their slab down into bigger rocks than others. Some trappers where more flexible with payments arrangements and set up payment plans that aloud smokers to buy crack with a promise to pay with in an agreed time frame. The lowly crackheads were there to buy crack but if a smoker was in the trap he was conducting business same as the trapper. Every consumer wants the most bang for his buck. A crackhead is no different.

Liberty, Texas was small. Very small, so all the trappers were either a child hood friend or a relative of mine, and the junkies were no strangers either. When business would slow some of my friends and family who were at work would gravitate toward the car I was perched on to kill time. When we weren't talking shit or cracking jokes I would be prodded into telling stories about life in Georgia. The only experience that most of people in Texas had with Georgia was what they saw in videos, and everyone wanted to know if what they were seeing was legit. BET had branded ATL as the mecca for black people, and everyone had bought into it. I was no different.

I did my best to paint verbal pictures of life in Hinesville and Savannah to those who were intrigued. I broke down the differences in living and surviving in low country Georgia compared to Texas. The stories of how black people were getting money, living in huge brick houses, and driving foreign cars made jaws drop and heads shake. It was unbelievable to them as it had been to me. I told stories of visiting my two aunts in Atlanta and all the riches I had witnessed in the black mecca. The stories were easy to tell because I didn't have to make anything up. I was telling the truth.

I sat on that car for what seemed like hours taking mental note after note. My wheels spent at full throttle. The game looked too easy. I was going to be in Texas all summer I might as well make some money while I was there. As I sat on that car the decision was been made and I anxious to get started. I had seen enough and was minutes from going back into the trailer to by a $50 slab from the big cat.

Sometimes God doesn't like what he sees in your heart and he sends you a sign. Almost at the exact moment of my decision everything suddenly changed.

Out the corner of my eye I got a glimpse of a man briskly walking toward the trap. After a few seconds the blurry image became crystal clear. I realized who it was. It was one of my dad's brothers and he was headed straight towards me sitting in the trap. As I slow made out his face the look I saw meant business. "What the Fuck!"

Here I was, caught red handed in the trap with one of my uncles about to run up on me and my cousin. I wasn't sure on how it was play out, but I was positive there was about to be a confrontation with my uncle. There were only a couple of ways the situation could end. One, he would try to snatch us up and get physical. Two, he would attempt to scold us and run us off from the trap Three, he would scold us and then snitch on us to our fathers, and then hell would really break loose.

I glanced over to see if H had got wind of the approaching situation. As normal, H was already on top of things. The look on his face had let me know he had noticed my uncle before I had but how he was reacting wasn't matching how I was thinking. He stared right at our uncle and didn't flinch or look concerned one bit. His face seemed to grow angrier the closer my uncle got. My uncle and H simultaneously started heading toward where I was perched on the broke down car. H and my uncle met up half way right in front of the car.

The last time I had an uncle confront me about my dealings in the streets it didn't go well. As I maneuvered threw the streets of Liberty, Texas I felt protected and watched over to a certain extent. I didn't want the special treatment, but I can't pretend as if I didn't notice it. It was as if the males on both sides of my family saw something worth preserving in me and took a special interest in making sure I for filled my potential. If need be on occasion they would come down on me with physical force if they caught me engaging in something that could compromise me.

The ushering of my potential wasn't limited to my legitimate uncles. My illegitimate uncles seemed to keep the closest watch over me. Wolf and Brian played major roles in making sure I understood my boundaries. Almost a decade before Wolf, one of my grandfather Joe's sons outside of his marriage ran up on me in the street and I never forgot the outcome. Wolf had caught me red handed in the middle of a dice game. I was no older than 10, but dice games weren't anything I was a stranger to. They were so common on The Lane that I didn't know they were frowned upon. I was in the middle of a dice game on one knee shaking the dice by my ear just like I saw the older hustlers do when Wolf seemed to appear out of nowhere. He snatched me off my knees and out of the dice game before I had chance to make a run for it.

After he snatched me out the game he proceeded to jack me up by my neck against the side of the house I had been playing against. He then informed me of the consequences I would face if he caught me again. Since he was limited to what he could do to me physically without upsetting my pops he did the next best thing. He snitched me out to my dad. About a day later my dad my dad was back at the house after working one of his four days on four day off tours. He called me in early out the street. Unaware Wolf had snitched on me I went into the house to talk with dad with my guard down. Before I could get both feet in the house good he had already taken his belt off.

At the time my uncle approached me in the trap sitting on that car I was 16 and full grown in my opinion. I felt grown and responsible for my own decisions but I still maintained the same amount of respect for my uncles that I had possessed as a child. Before I could make my mind up on how I was going to play this with my uncle I got a clear glimpse in his eyes. It was all clear all of a sudden. There wasn't the fire of anger that I expected to see. His eyes were blood shot and glossed over. I was expected the look of displeasure to meet my gaze but instead I was met with a look of humbleness. This nigga hadn't run up on us to shut us down. He was a smoker, and he had come to do business.

To my surprise, my uncle was so focused in on what he came to do that he barely acknowledged my presence. He made a beeline straight to H. "Jr., let me talk to you. I ain't gone lie; all I got is $3 on me right now. Nephew I need a favor from you. Can you cut me down a $3 rock?"

H just stared straight through him as if he didn't hear a word my uncle had just said. My uncle caught on fast that Plan A wasn't working and switched right to Plan B.

"Nephew, tell you what, take this $3 I got give me a $5 piece, and I'll bring you back the other $2 later today."

Before my uncle could finish his second proposal H switched gears and went to a place I had rarely seen him go. H cut my uncle in the middle of his words. "Nigga!! What I told you about that shit? I don't cut any mutha-fuckin rocks down. What the fuck you think this is?"

My uncle went to talk and H cut him off again. "I'll tell you what you can do nigga. Take yo' ass away from here and go get $2 mo' and then bring yo' ass back"

My uncle started loading up to plead his case again but before he could get a single word out his mouth H was on his ass again. "Nigga, I just told you what I had to say and you're getting close to making me mad."

My uncle looked down at his feet and his shoulders drooped. My uncle turned and walked away. He was gone just as fast as he had come.

My ambition for selling crack in the city most of my family had been raised in had taken a hit. If I wanted to sell crack in Liberty I would have to shit on my own kinfolks to be successful. That was something I wasn't built to do. God had spoken to me, I heard, and I understood. H and I would do a lot of things together but hand to hand trapping in Liberty, Texas wouldn't be one of them.

# BLOOD IN MY MOUTH

The dope game wasn't for me at the time. That put an end to the idea of H and me getting money together that summer. Chasing money wasn't our main objective at that age anyway. Getting money was only a means to an end. The end game was always broads. We measured our self-worth and our quality of life on how many women we had acquired and had on deck.

At that age everything we did pertained to our primary goal of acquiring more women. I didn't want to wear fashionable clothes because I had a need to feel pretty. I wore fashionable clothes because it made women more attracted to me. I didn't chase money because I wanted to have a big pile of green paper I could lay on. I chased money because having more disposable income meant I could buy more things that would attract women.

In ga, my rotation of young girls I dealt with was three or four girls deep and I was considered a pretty good player. In Texas, H was on another level. He had three or four girls in every neighborhood. H was limited to the city of Liberty either. It seemed as if H had at least one girl in every city within a 15-mile radius of Liberty. There was obviously a huge distance between our ability to pull women and I was aware of it so I piggy backed off H's game.

I could pull my own women but it was easier to let H set me up. Liberty was the country and girls were of a limited supply. Most guys were lucky to have two or three on deck, but the rules didn't apply to us. Every day it we were posting up and trying to make out with two or three different sets of girls.

Life was perfect, I was back home and everything in my world was in order. I had plenty of money, plenty of women, and plenty of free time to do as I pleased. With everything going so smoothly I dropped my guard. Liberty was home and I was amongst family again. I became so comfortable I got sloppy. Through all my travels I had learned to never let my guard down and to never get comfortable. Something about being home made me ignore the rules that had kept me safe. I would have to pay the mental lapse.

One night H and I were out wasting gas and killing time when we ended up making a stop at his main girl's home on the river. His main girl was a skinny petite little thing but possessed a super fly mouth. She was to slim for my taste but that attitude she displayed made her sexy. Slim had her own ride and a steady job. She was doing pretty well for a young girl from the hood.

When we pulled up to her house on the river there were a couple cars already parked in the yard. H either knew the cars or didn't care who were in them but he didn't hesitate to knock on the door. He knocked a few times and when nobody answered he walked right in.

After we walked through the door unannounced we found three males and H's girl in the living room with the TV blasting. The loud TV had drowned the sound of H knocking on the door. When we appeared out of nowhere, they were obviously startled. Two guys I saw sitting on one couch smoking were related to me. I hadn't run into them that summer so we greeted each other and started catching up. The third a guy I didn't know, but it was apparent he had some dealings with Slim by the way he acted around H. He was fidgety because he wasn't sure if he had been caught red handed trying to pull off a creep. The thing about H was he probably was hip to what he had walked in on, but he didn't care because he really didn't try to own any of his women.

While I was catching up with my kinfolk H and Slim went into her bedroom and shut the door behind them. I wasn't sure if they wanted to talk in private about us walking in on her with a house full of niggas or if he was going to try and put some work in. Regardless, my two cousins that had been smoking a sweet on the couch and the unknown guy realized that it was time for them to break camp.

On the way out the door one of my cousins that we had walked in on asked if I wanted to hang out with them. I politely declined his offer, but in my mind I thought, "Hell fuck nawl!" There were three great reasons to turn him down. The first was them niggas liked to get wet. Getting wet meant they dipped cigarettes and sweets into formaldehyde and then smoked that shit. Getting wet was probably the most low-key shit they did, and I wasn't interested in finding out how they got down when they really wanted to get loose. The second was I didn't trust the third guy. He gave me a bad vibe and that was enough for me. The third was that I wanted to get out. If H didn't come out that room in an hour, I would take the truck and go prowling by myself. Staying put was a no-brainer.

My kinfolk and the unknown guy went about their business and left me to myself at Slim's house. I settled in on the couch and figured I would to take the opportunity to take a quick nap. I wasn't getting much sleep and this was the perfect opportunity to catch up. I had turned off the lights in the living room and laid down on the couch. But before I could drift off I thought I heard something scat across the floor. A few seconds later I felt something run under the couch I was sitting on.

I was from the country but I still was uncomfortable with certain creatures. I heard too many stories about the rats and the urban legend was that they were as big as cats and they would bite. The prospect of being bitten shook me. There was no way in hell I was leaving my feet on the ground in harm's way. I put my feet on the couch, dirty Nikes and all. I wasn't raised to blatantly disrespect other people's belongings, but I wasn't going to leave my feet exposed to get chewed on.

I laid on the couch with my feet up for what seemed like a couple of hours. I would doze off for a few minutes and then wake back up in fear of that rat. The last time I dozed off I was awaken by a different sounding noise. This time it came from the door. I heard somebody outside fumbling with door trying to get it open. I jumped up out that couch and onto my feet. I conducted a quick scan of the room searching for something I use as weapon. I didn't have a clue of who could have been at the door at this time of night but it could have been another one of Slim's niggas. I didn't want to be run up on empty handed.

Before I could find anything to pick up the door flung open.

My nerves calmed down after I saw who was standing in the door. It was slims younger sister and she was caring her small son in one of her arms. She drunkenly stumbled her way into the house. Her eyes were good and glossed over. We spoke and I briefly explained to her why I was on their couch. We skipped the introductions because she was no stranger. We had known each other since middle school.

"You straight? You look like you went and got full?" Not that I really cared, but I felt obligated to check on her since she was holding a baby.

She slurred back, "I just came from a little get-together and had a little to drink, but I'm ok." She stumbled into the house and started heading toward her room.

A light bulb went off in my head. I had always been attracted to the girl but she was too fast and ran with too many niggas. At the moment none of that mattered. I had seen an opportunity. This broad had lied; she hadn't had a little bit to drink. She had had a lot of bit to drink. With the wisdom I have gained through the years I know a half-drunk strange woman is something to run from, but at the time I was 16. At that young age a half-drunk woman looks like an open gate to a wild horse. I was about run right threw her.

I offered to walk her to her room to make sure she got the baby in the crib and didn't knock over any walls. She looked me in my eyes and the look on her face let me know she knew what I was up to. She agreed and we headed down the hall to her room. After we made our way to her room she laid her sleeping baby in his crib. He was in a deep sleep and never batted an eye the entire time I was in the room with his mama. After she sat the baby down she fumbled over to the corner of the bed where I had taken a seat.

After a short conversation I convinced her she needed a back massages. To my surprise, things were going smoothly. I worked my hands all over her back and shoulders making sure to grab her tight and deep. I wanted her to feel the power in my hands. After a few minutes she started moaning and rolling her neck. The combination of my hands and that liquor she had drunk earlier was too much for her to fight. I wasn't sure of how much time I had before H came out of Slim's room and broke up my party so I made a move.

I moved in and ran my tongue across her neck before I started to kiss up and down the side of her neck. I had run my game to perfection. After a few seconds of sucking on her I ran my hands across her thighs and when she jumped up. "Hold on for a sec. Let me go to the bathroom and clean up a lil bit." She got up and made her way to the bathroom.

She shut the door behind her and a few seconds later I heard running water. I could hear her splashing around in the sink taking a bird bath. After a minute or two the bathroom door opened and she stumbled back to the bed barely making it. While she was getting ready in the bathroom I was doing the same. In my palm was a rubber I had already taken out of the plastic. Girls had a bad habit of going back and forth with their decisions so if she gave me the green light I was going to move fast. I wouldn't give her a chance to second guess her decision.

I glanced at her half-drunken body lying in that bed and I held my breath, hoping that she didn't flake out on me. Before I could put my hands back and attempt to pull her clothes she had started trying to undress herself. As she fumbled with her clothes it became ever more obvious that liquor she had drank was winning.

Time was against me, so I picked up the pace trying to get us both naked. I moved as quickly as I could because I didn't want her to tap out, and I didn't want Slim and H to know I had crept on Slim's sister. After we were finally both naked I didn't waste any time. I propped her up on a couple of pillows and got behind her. I fumbled for a few seconds with the condom but managed to get it on before wasting too much time. Before I could half way penetrate the girl she fell asleep. It took a lot of will power but I walked away from the situation cold turkey. Going at her while she was sleep wasn't worth the risk.

Damn, I was so close. Horridly, I put back on my clothes and I crept out her room and headed back toward the couch trying not to make too much noise. But before I could get both of my feet out of the bedroom door way, Slim's bedroom door flung open and H caught me red-handed creeping.

He looked at me and said something in such a low tone I couldn't make it out. He smirked, shook his head, and went back in Slim's bedroom. H and I were as close as they come, but I still preferred to keep a lot of things I did to myself. Trying to creep on Slim's sister was one of them. I had good reason to want to keep that business to myself and I never confirmed or denied what happen to anyone. That was my business.

Word on street was that there were two possible fathers to my creep partner's baby. The baby belonged to the big cat from the trailer or Chrome. Chrome was one of H and GB's maternal cousins, and he was also one of my little sister's uncles. To say the least we were very familiar with each other. He didn't currently live on The Lane but his grandparents and his father use to live off The Lane same as mine. He was a descendent of 563, same as me. Like everybody else my age around Liberty Chrome was a trapper. Similar to Youngsta, Chrome was rumored to have a set of hands equal to mine.

Two or three days passed and I didn't put any more thought into my dealings with the drunken girl. Nothing had become of the situation and I wasn't interested in pursuing it any further. I also didn't think anything of it because the girl wasn't claimed outright by anybody so I didn't consider making a play on her a violation.

At that young age I was going through a cold and hard spell. I had no thoughts of creating emotional attachments to women. I assumed since everybody I knew was in the street they were just as heartless and loveless towards women as I was. A woman was a means to an end. I needed women to entertain me and bring me a physical pleasure. I had no other needs or desires.

A few days had gone by and I was on The Lane as usual. There was nothing special about the day and I had spent most of my time waiting for the sun to go down. While killing time I ran into my cousin GB. H's little brother. We hadn't talked much since my arrival home for the summer. I had a couple of beers in me but I was in the presence of family so I was as comfortable as I could be. After a few minutes and few jokes the beer told me it would be funny to tell a small portion of the story my adventure with the drunken girl. I didn't tell him exact details just enough to have a laugh. We had our small laugh and then we were both on our way.

That night I ended up hanging out with one of my uncles. We spent our time drinking, playing dominoes, and talking shit for what seemed like hours. My uncle dropped me off back on The Lane half drunk around 2 a.m. It was only 2 a.m. but it felt much earlier. A full moon was out so the normally pitch black country lane was well lit.

There was always something going on at H's mama house so I took the short walk from my grandmother's house down the street to hang out with my cousins. I tapped on the back door twice out of courtesy and walked in. Their door was never locked just like everybody else that lived on The Lane. After I entered the house and walked through the kitchen I encountered GB and I spoke with him briefly. Something was off. I didn't know exactly what was up, but he seemed distant. I didn't think anything of it and kept moving. As soon I cut around the corner and entered the living room I ran into Chrome sitting on a couch. I spoke and he spoke back but it wasn't normal. We didn't mix words but I could feel the tension coming from him. There was no dapping up or other normal hood greeting. Instead it was more like a sizing up. Chrome and I had a problem.

The greeting made me uneasy because I knew what it was. Neither Chrome nor I would ever disrespect our Aunt's house by getting into it, so I continued to where I was headed. I walked through the back of the house and down the hall way back to H's room. He was laid out on the bed staring up at the ceiling listen to DJ Screw and Tupac mixtape.

"What's good, kinfolk?"

I replied, "Ain't nothing" and laid on the floor beside his bed and joined him staring up at the ceiling.

A couple of days earlier when I was trying to con that drunken broad out of her drawers, it dawned on me I might be stepping on some toes. Stepping created beef. Chrome was clearly under the impression I had knocked off his baby mama. He handled beef no different than I did. There wasn't going to be a discussion to clear things up. We didn't talk beef out. As I laid half drunk on H's bedroom floor I tried to focus and sober up. I knew what was coming next.

I didn't get a chance to lie on the floor and focus for long before Chrome was at H's room door. He started talking and I didn't listen to anything he said or even look at him. I just continued to stare up at the ceiling. I knew what time it was. H jumped to his feet out of his bed. He was caught off guard, but I wasn't. All H knew was he had a cousin from both sides of his family about to square off.

Chrome didn't mix words with me. He got straight to the point. He was talking so fast I couldn't decipher much of what he was saying but I caught when he called me to the square.

"Say, cuz, I'm not going to disrespect my aunt's house. You and I need to go outside." My heart started racing and my mouth got dry. It was time to fight or fight. There were no other options when a man got called out.

The comfort of being home fooled me into letting my guard down and I had gotten sloppy. Texas was no different than Colorado. Texas was no different than Kansas. Texas was no different than Georgia. The rules still applied. The girl had choose, the haters had hated, and now it was time to lock up. Things went in that exact order, they always had and they always would.

Before I could stand up good H was attempting to play the role of peace maker. I stopped him before he could get started. "Naw, kinfolk, I got it. Let's take it outside."

We filed out the house single file. Chrome first with H and GB separating us. It was close to 3 a.m. and The Lane was empty and quiet. It was nice and peaceful like the calm before a big storm. This would be a true test of warriors. There would be no crowds to incite or boost us up. There would only be me and Chrome and H and GB to witness it. When we lined up in the street H stood between us and was trying to sort the situation out. The situation didn't need sorting out. I had tried to smash his baby mama and he called me out. There was no turning back. We would have to lock up now or we would lock up later but one thing was for sure we had to lock up. If something didn't happen both of our reputations would take a hit. People would think both of us were soft. The best thing to do was to get it over with.

I had been drinking for almost three straight days and my senses were numb. I felt slow and could barely stand up straight but it didn't matter. It wasn't like I could ask Chrome to give me a day or two to sober up and prepare. I stood there in the street quietly readying myself for the clash. H and Chrome were doing most of the talking. I didn't want to waste any energy going back and forth; my only focus was on trying to gain my bearings. During all the exchanging of words I was so far off my game that I didn't notice Chrome slowly inching closer and closer to me. H was attempting to keep himself between us trying to sort things out to avoid the physical confrontation. The rules were the rules and H couldn't prevent the inevitable. Under my radar Chrome had been inching closer and closer to striking distance. He kept his hands to his sides and my numb senses failed to alert me to the danger I was in.

There wasn't much difference in size between Chrome and me. We were about the same height and same build but he had about a 10-pound muscular advantage. He was wiry, strong, and quick. It would have been a heavy order to subdue him if I were sober, and here I was half drunk. The streets wouldn't care about excuses if I took an ass whipping drunk or sober. My reputation was built on me being a fearless street fighter but it didn't matter how many fights I had won. All it would take was one lost and my aura of indestructibility would be gone.

I put my hand up to my mouth and tasted the warm salty blood that poured from my front teeth. Chrome had caught me with a straight right. He threw the punch from his hip and I never saw it coming. The punch was quick, mean and was so accurate it still impresses me to this day. I'm not sure how he did it because H was standing between us, it was dark, and I was drunk. He must have taken a quick step to his right and side threw the punch simultaneously. It landed in my mouth perfectly.

It wasn't a dishonorable act to sucker punch me. It's part of the game. What upset me was that I had let him get the jump on me. I had made a name from firing off punches at unsuspecting angles at unsuspecting people. Chrome had just been beat at my own game. It had been so long since I had been punched first it shocked me. As soon as he hit me with the punch I recoiled back from the power of the blow. After the brief shock of the punch I immediately tried to shoot the gap between H and Chrome.

Before I could launch myself into Chrome and return his aggression I felt myself being snatched off the ground and carried away. H had me locked in a bear hug and he carried me off. He held me so tight in his grip it felt as if he was crushing me. GB grabbed Chrome in similar fashion.

As he carried me away from the fight I pleaded with H to let me go. "Please cuz, let me go. You can't let me go out like this." At the time I was so angry that I couldn't finish the fight I could feel my eyes well up. H knew I was drunk and in no condition to fight. He was protecting me from an ass whipping. He knew more than likely I would have taken an ugly loss that night and as much as I don't like to admit it I knew the same thing. He saved me.

That night Chrome was fighting for his honor and with his heart. He disrespected by my trying to lay up with his baby mama. In the same breath I was drunk and had nothing to fight for but pride. But when he punched me in my mouth like a chump something clicked inside of me.

All the commotion must have woken up my aunt and she came outside and asked what was going on. Snitching was unheard of. "Ain't nothing going on. We were just out here messing around."

The conflicted ended there and I took the long walk back toward my grandmother's house. My mouth continuously filled up with blood as I walked home. I traced my tongue across my teeth and I felt what made me as mad as I ever had been to that date. Chrome had almost knocked out my two top front teeth. One tooth was loose enough to wiggle a little and the other was hanging by a thread.

After I finished the lonely walk to my grandmother's house I headed straight into the bathroom. I stood over the toilet and spit all the blood that was leaking from my mouth into the water. I stared at the dark red clots and pink water for what seemed like an hour. This had not just happened to me. I had never known what it felt like to be backed down. I had never known what it felt like to feel inferior. Chrome had awakened me up with one punch, and everything I thought about myself was up for questioning.

I left the bath room and entered my bedroom. I sat on the corner of my bed. The conflict had sobered me up and I was too amped to sleep. As I sat on the corner of the corner of my bed I stared at my reflection in the mirror. As I gazed at my reflection I worked my loose teeth over again and again with my tongue. The more I stared the less I liked myself. I looked at my body and for the first time in my life I saw myself for what I was. I was no gladiator, I wasn't indestructible. I was a short, frail, half-breed-looking, curly-headed little boy.

# REBIRTH

Every day I walked the street with men but I still had the physique of a 13 year old boy. I was well aware that there were many of my peers that were waiting on a chance to take a shot at me. My reputation had kept them at bay but my reputation had taken a hit. I had survived in the streets were the skinny niggas perish for years off an iron. My iron will wouldn't be enough anymore. Chrome had exposed me and soon the wolves would be at my doorstep.

The morning after Chrome punched me in the mouth I stared in that mirror for hours as I held my tooth in place with my tongue. Thoughts of revenge on my mind. Girls, money, sex, and returning to Georgia would stay on hold until I had my redemption. I wanted nothing else but a chance to square off with Chrome. If I was going to square up with him things would be different the second time. I would need to reinvent myself. I feel asleep staring in that mirror tasting the constant stream of blood leak into my mouth. I didn't sleep long.

I woke up after only a few hours of sleep with a newfound passion. After rising from the brief sleep I got up and closed my bedrooms door. I laid on the floor in front of my bed and began to train like a man possessed. Sit up after sit up, push up after push up, that's how I would give birth to the new Larry M. Brooks. After strapping ankle weights to my wrist I began to shadow boxed in the mirror. Five-minute sessions of shadowboxing followed up by 35 reps of closed-hand pushups.

After an hour or two my grandmother came to my bedroom door curious to the source of all the noise leaking from under the door. She gave the door a couple of light knocks and pushed it open. "Monte', is everything all right?"

"Yes, ma'am, I'm just working out a little bit."

"Well, I cooked breakfast. There are some grits and eggs on the stove." She responded in sweet, mothering way.

"I'm all right grandma. I'm not hungry right now, but I might get some later." I was too focused to eat and I couldn't eat at the time if I wanted to. My teeth were in no condition to chew up food. I continued my routine in the room all morning. Pushups, sit-ups, and shadowboxing. I only stopped for water and restroom breaks.

After three or four hours I bored with my routine. I left my room and went next door to my uncle Yogi's house. My uncle slept during the day because he worked the 3rd shift. Socializing wasn't my mission anyway. His door was unlocked so I entered his house and retrieved the key to his shed. In the shed behind his house he kept an old curl bar and a dusty bench with a rusty bar. I was no stranger to working out with weights but I had never seen in results or changes in my body. It was because I never had put my heart into working out. My heart and everything else I had was into it now. After locking myself in that shed I worked out so long I lost track of time.

I stayed in the shed until I couldn't feel my arms any longer. The entire time I worked out I held my tooth locked in place with my tongue. Every time I felt that tooth wiggle it would rekindle my anger and that would restore my energy. I was exhausted but my anger kept me training like an animal. My embarrassment also kept me in that shed. No one knew where I was so no one could find me and force me to confront the night before.

For three days and three nights I didn't go any further than my bedroom or that shed to work out. I avoided everybody. I hadn't had a drink while I was training and I barely ate because of my tooth. A purification of my body was an unplanned side effect of not putting much into my system. After a few days my tooth started to lock back in and all the working out and shadowboxing had paid dividends on my psyche. Privately, I admired all the new tiny little veins running down my arms from all the training. I could feel myself growing stronger. After three days of solitude I had sobered up and I had restored some of the confidence in myself that Chrome had robbed me of.

After three days I was ready. Ready to go back into the streets. Ready to reestablish myself. Ready to restore my honor. The wolves were coming and I was ready for that as well. My first day back, I stumbled upon a group of guys hanging out under a shade tree playing dominoes. One of the guys under the shade tree was my uncle. Brian Bankhead, the knock out artist. As a youngster, he had coerced me into countless fights and conflicts. He spent a lot of his time training me up and I was ashamed when I saw him. The city was small. It would have been impossible for him to have not heard I had got my mouth bled.

I sat and watched the game being played out for a few minutes. I anticipated that someone would call me out. Nobody mentioned my previous conflict or asked any questions about what had happened. They carried on with their normal conversations like they weren't aware of the conflict until Brian acknowledged the elephant in the room.

"Man, I don't know why they held you back. They should have turned you loose so you could have gotten in that nigga's ass."

"That would have been a good fight." Someone at the table added his two cents to what Brian was saying.

Brian knew my confidence had been shaken and he was trying to ease the tension I had brewing inside of me. I didn't say anything back as he spoke. All I could do was shake my head in acknowledgement as I stared down at my feet. I kept my head down as he spoke because I could feel my eyes watering up in embarrassment and anger. I didn't know what to do with all the pent up rage inside of me so I left the table and returned to the shed. I needed a second shot at Chrome.

In secret I kept up my intense training regimen during the early mornings. I didn't want the word to get out that I was creating an edge for myself. I didn't want Chrome to know that he was on a crash course with something so angry and intense that maybe he would be shaken. I wanted him to maintain the old image of me. The last thing I wanted was to scare him into training and preparing for me.

I had an edge and I kept the knowledge of my training to myself. The shadowboxing paid huge dividends.

Throwing hundreds of punches with ankle weights on my risk had improved my hand speed. I had improved to the point where I couldn't see my hands moving when I punched with the weights off. I was going to pick his as apart.

I worked out and shadow boxed for so many hours I could feel myself turning into a machine. My body had never felt so in tune. My hands were becoming quicker and quicker. I felt beautiful as I gazed at my reflection in the mirror as I shadowboxed. When I let my hands fly in that mirror it would cause me to smirk because I could see how far I had come. Chrome hadn't a clue what was coming for him. I had learned how to channel my all my anger into training my body. It was a lesson I kept with me for a life time.

After a few weeks of the intense training my confidence was restored and surpassed where it once was. I patiently awaited my chance to go toe to toe with Chrome. The thoughts consumed me and not a minute went by that I didn't think of him bleeding my mouth and stripping me of my reputation. He wouldn't be back on The Lane anytime soon because he knew I would be gunning for him. I would have to go out and find him.

A few weeks had gone by and everything was back to normal. I didn't venture off The Lane as much. I was ok with training and hanging out around the hood. One late night on The Lane we got a small crap game going in the street. We were almost right in front of my Grandmother Ellen's house, but it was late so it didn't matter. Anyone who would have cared was sleep. It was me a few kinfolk and another cat I grew up with on The Lane, Bubba.

Physically, Bubba was about 20 or 30 pounds bigger than me and at least three inches taller. Socially he was into the street life pretty deep and he was known for maintaining a constant high on some of the harder drugs. In the hood we said he used those drugs as an excuse to play crazy with white folks. The hood knew he wasn't crazy.

The crap game was going good for me. I was cleaning up and mainly profiting off Bubba. His facial expressions hinted that my relieving him of his money wasn't sitting well with him but that's the name of the game. After I had him down about $50 he said the strangest thing straight to my face. After he crapped out again, I was reaching down to grab my latest winnings when the nigga let the last thing he should have ever said fall out his mouth.

"Nigga, I ought to steal you in your mouth like Chrome did."

Just like I had predicted. The wolves sensed blood. Niggas who wouldn't have thought twice about trying me would now be trying me on a daily basis. He now saw me as soft. His words actually didn't upset me, I was glad he called me out. This was a good thing for me. Bubba would be a warm up to see where I was at before I faced off with Chrome.

After Bubba mumbled his insults at me he didn't even bother to look me in the face. He kept his head down focusing in on the crap game like he didn't just disrespect me to the third power. I didn't even bother standing straight up. Still squatting in my dice shooting position I shot that nigga a left jab straight to the middle of his face. He fell and landed on his ass. I could have stole on him with a right and tried to knock him out with the first punch, but I didn't want to end the fight early. I wanted to show any one watching what the hell I was about. He wasn't Chrome but I would punish this nigga just like he was.

After I sucker punched Bubba I stood up and took a couple of steps back from him. I gave him time to gather himself and get off the ground. After he got up and on his feet he stared at me with the look of a killer. It didn't matter. I had no fear in me. I had never been so well prepared for a conflict in life. I didn't even bother to put my hands up to guard my face or raise them in a fighting position. I was going to disrespect this nigga and fight him with my hands at my hips. He was no threat to me and I wanted him and everyone else watching to know.

Bubba quickly charged in on me and threw a couple of wild punches. He threw a right and then a left hook with everything he had. I ducked the first punch he threw and I bobbed my head backwards to dodge the second punch. He was off balance from the wild punches he threw so I took advantage the situation and unloaded a two punch combo to his face. After the combo I gave him a shove to create some distance between us. I wasn't about to let him grab me. This fight was going to stay standing up where I could control it.

I could hear the spectators go "ooh" and "aww" as I toyed with Bubba. I was going to turn the fight into a show. I didn't want to just beat Bubba I wanted to humiliate him. This would be a warning and a display.

Bubba wasn't badly hurt by my combo, but the look on his face showed he was steaming. He had eaten three punches but hadn't managed to lay a hand on me despite his effort. He stopped and just stared at me thinking over his game plan. As he stood still I danced a circle around him. Purposely I kept my hands down and smiled at him to display as much disrespect as possible. I could see his frustration steadily building. It was time to throw salt in his wounds.

"Steal me in the mouth like Chrome?" I laughed. "Faggot-ass nigga. I'm going to beat your ass until I get tired."

My talking during the middle of our fight went straight through his heart and hit his pride. He charged in and made an attempt to grab me. I side step his efforts and unloaded another punch to his face. He still hadn't put his hands on me and I was picking him off at will. After that last exchange it was obvious Bubba was over matched. The hood stepped in to put an end to the shut out. A couple of my kinfolks grabbed Bubba and H grabbed me and that ended the conflict.

As H carried me out of the fight to a neutral spot he looked at me like with a face that told me he knew the old Larry was back. He put me down a few yards from where the fight had taken place. He didn't have to worry about holding me back from returning to the fight. I had accomplished what I had set out to do. I looked over at Bubba and I smiled at him again to add injury to insult. He was so frustrated tears started to pour down his face.

"Fuck you nigga, I got something for you. You have to walk your ass down the street to your grandma's house. I'll be waiting with my shotgun nigga."

Damn! Now that was some shit I didn't expect to hear. After everything calmed down, a couple of my kinfolks showed Bubba up street back toward his house. As I watched him angrily walk up the street I could hear him screaming crazy shit and going ape kicking things as he made his way home. Was that fool serious about shooting me? He was a little on the crazy side and everybody had accesses to a shotgun in the country.

Later that night after everything settled down and all the fun ended I had to walk home alone. To get to my grandmother's house I had to walk past Bubba's house. To say I was nervous was an understatement. When I got about two houses down from Bubba's house and I took off running. I zigzagged until I reached my grandmothers porch. I didn't feel completely safe until I was completely in the house. For the next few days, I would run and zigzag every time I had to go past it Bubba's house. I didn't know anybody who could whoop a bullet's ass.

At my grandmother's house I stumbled upon my brother and his running mate, Booby Trap, in the garage. They were smoking cigarettes and just hanging out. My brother was only 15. I had recently turned 17 and held the role of authority figure. I walked up on him and looked him in the face.

"What the fuck are you doing?" He looked kind of shaky and nervous but before he could reply Booby Trap answered for him.

"Nigga, it ain't none of your business what we out here doing. We are grown."

I looked at my brother and the fear had left his face. I glanced over at Booby and there was no fear in his face either. I could whip either one of these boys by themselves, but they had learned something that summer. They had finally figured out as a team I couldn't see them. Booby and my brother both stared at me like they were waiting on me to make a move. I bowed out. My brother was grown and I stayed out his business as much as I could from that day moving forward. Besides, I wasn't in the mood to take an ass whipping in that garage.

A couple of days passed without any events and I continued to train every morning before anybody woke up. My grandmother was the only person that had a clue what I was doing. She would see me enter into that shed every morning like clockwork.

Two weeks passed and I had started hanging in the streets with H again. One night while we were killing time he told me the strangest thing.

"Kinfolk Chrome wants to talk with you."

I respected and I trusted H so I didn't even question if it was a set up or something questionable. I simply replied "Okay."

H took me down to where Chrome stayed and he was outside waiting for us on the porch when we pulled up. I eyed him over when we pulled into the yard. Chrome didn't have the look of conflict in his face. It was more a look of humbleness and peace. He walked up on me looking me in my eyes and then held his hand out to dap me. Not fully trusting him I dapped him and then he told me what he had to say.

Chrome went to talking in his trademark fast pimp talk. "Kinfolk, I was fucked up for bringing that beef to you. That broad chose you. Broads are going to be broads, and players are going to be players. Cuz I'm sorry for stealing on you. That was a hoe move."

As he spoke I listened and let go of all my hate and animosity. I gained a lot of respect for him because I knew it took a man to do what he was doing.

He could have let the beef stand and we could have did battle over and over in the street, but he manned up and humbled himself. That allowed us to put the beef to bed. I didn't let him do all the talking by himself either. He wasn't all to blame for our beef. I was wrong for putting myself in the situation with his baby mama and I admitted that I deserved to get my mouth bled. I had plenty girls to choose from, I had no business crossing swords with another man from my hood over his baby's mama.

After the talk we all went and got a bottle of Thunderbird. We drank and talked shit like the beef never happened. Later that night we to a drive to Jack in the Box and Chrome went into his pocket and fed everybody in the car. Peace had been restored in my world.

After peace was restored I left Liberty and went to Houston and spent the rest of the summer running wild with my uncle D-Ray. Before we had squashed the beef, I had turned down D-Ray to come hang out in Houston. I knew if I left the block and went to the city before the beef was handled I would look like a coward. As long as we had beef I wouldn't have left Liberty under any circumstance not even to return to Georgia. My honor was restored so I was free to move around as I pleased again.

# THE SYSTEM

The summer in Texas had come and gone. I was back in Georgia with a mind full of stories about the adventures I had participated in to tell my friends. There were only a few weeks left of my summer. In a few days I would start my final year of high school. Life in Texas was never far from my heart, but I didn't belong there anymore. The life I wanted to build as a man was evolving.

I hadn't been back in Georgia 24 hours before I linked up with my running mate, Nic. To celebrate my return he set up my favorite pastime. He made a call and within an hour we were kicking it with his ex, Shante, and one of her friends. There weren't many places for teenagers to hang out in Hinesville, so we usually killed time hanging out in front of someone's house.

Today was no different. Nic, the girls, and I posted up in an empty lot across the street from my house. We leaned on my car and listened to music and enjoyed the hot Georgia evening. I was the first out of my crew to purchase a car. Just like my bike had been before my car was my new symbol of freedom.

Timmy V had taken the savings I had left under my mother's watch while I was in Texas and bought me an old school. My first ride was a faded brown '83 Pontiac Bonneville. I wasn't too fond of the car at first, because

I didn't like the fact that Timmy V left me out of the purchasing process. It was my money so I should have had some kind of say on what car my money purchased.

Another problem I had with the Bonneville was Timmy V had pulled a bait and switch on me. While I was in Texas he had sold me on a dream that he was going to take my saved money and help me get me purchase a new Ford Ranger. Prior to Timmy V getting involved with purchasing a car for me something lit a fire under him. That same summer in Texas my dad purchased a candy red, convertible Mustang and gave it to me for my 17th birthday.

Not wanting to be out shined Timmy V suddenly started aggressively pursuing helping me purchase a car. My dad giving me the Mustang must have made Timmy V uncomfortable. When word got back to him about me bringing the Mustang back to Georgia, it became a huge issue. Needless to say I was forced to leave my "gift" Mustang in Texas and settle with the "hard-earned" Bonneville. I didn't stay salty for long; I had my own car.

I didn't want to come across ungrateful so I never let on to Timmy V that I was hip to the subplot. The Bonneville was cool, but as I leaned on my car with those girls I couldn't help but to wonder how many girls I could have pulled if I were pushing that candy red, convertible Mustang. That Mustang even had white leather seats. In the grand scheme of things my stepdad had probably meant well, but once again he had seriously hated on me.

Nic, the two girls and I had been hanging out in that empty lot for an hour or so when we started to faintly hear some loud talking approaching us from down the street. I took a peek in the direction the noise was generated. My senses went off; trouble was heading our way.

The neighborhood I lived in Hinesville was on the edge of town and isolated. It was rare to see strangers walking our streets, but one was on the street today. I had been away for a few months so I wasn't sure if the guy was new to the neighborhood and just wasn't familiar to me yet. This was our hood, but we weren't the type to give anyone a hard time just for passing through. Personally, I didn't look for trouble and I didn't want any, but this man was in our hood doing everything in his nature to draw negative attention to himself. I knew what it was going to be as the stranger made his way up my street.

As he got closer his words became legible. It was obvious what he was trying to do. He was trying to disrespect our neighborhood. He wanted to show us there wasn't anybody that lived in the two car garage brick houses that could match up with him.

The first words I made out from the stranger heading our way were, "Them bitches ain't fine! "I can take them hoes if I want 'em."

I was tired of confrontations. I had my fill of beef during my stay in Texas and really wanted the situation to blow over. In my mind I had a cowardly conversation with myself. "Well these really aren't my women. These are Nic's broads. It ain't my job to defend their honor."

As I glanced over at the two girls I could see they were becoming increasingly uncomfortable the closer the stranger got. The girls were in my hood to hang out with me and whether I liked it or not, they had become my responsibility. As the stranger approached us he became louder and more obnoxious the closer he got. We had no prior dealings with this man; therefore, his behavior was unprovoked. He assumed that Nic and I were soft and he needed to punk us.

I didn't include any of the other three of my thoughts because I wasn't sure how everything was going to play out. I wasn't too worried because I had an ace in the hole. As the stranger was approaching us from up the street I had made eye contact with my brother. He was doing yard work across the street in our front yard. Gene saw the situation and he knew the drill.

When the stranger entered range I took the opportunity to size him up. What I saw didn't make me feel good about the situation. As he approached us he had taken his shirt off. He was a beast. He was almost jailhouse swole. After seeing his size I started to have second thoughts about running up on this nigga. "Damn! This nigga is big; do I really want to do this?" The way he was boss hogging our neighborhood left me with no other option. He was in my neighborhood, and he was shitting on Nic and me in front of these girls. Those girls had to be thinking wondering if we were going to act like some hoes or man up.

If I made eye contact with the stranger I knew there would be no turning back. Fuck it. When he was close enough I looked him in his eyes, gave him a smirk, and then folded my arms across my chest. It was on now.

"Little nigga, don't know why you folding your arms like you got a problem. I'll knock your little red ass out."

Before he could finish calling me out, I raised up off the car. I instantly put my hand in fighting position like that nigga could have hit me from 30 feet. I started a slow walk towards him. My heart was beating a 1,000 times a minute. I prayed to God that my brother in the yard watching was going do what I planned he was going to do.

The stranger stood his ground and locked himself into a fighting position. Steadily with my hands up I eased my way towards him and closed the distance. My prayers were answered. My brother was closing the distance behind simultaneously as I closed it from the front. The stranger didn't have a clue he was about to be jumped. We were both only a few feet from locking up. My brother and I were about to use the Georgia boy style that had been used on me so many times over. I had never seen a one on one in Georgia and this nigga wasn't about to get one either. He had disrespected the entire neighborhood and my brother was part of the neighborhood. This would be an honor beating.

There was no turning back now. Right as before I entered arms range by luck the conflict was abruptly interrupted. A car came flying from the top of the street right at where we were about to lock up. The driver was hitting the horn and flashing the lights like crazy. The car came in so fast my adversary and I both had to jump out the street to avoid being run over.

The car spent to the side and out of the out of control car jumped my homeboy Davin. Davin was affiliated with certain local street organizations and was known to represent certain colors. Davin lived up the same street as I did and we had been cool since I moved to ga. He also knew the man who was trespassing and disrespecting. Davin mediated and squashed the beef between me and the stranger right there in the middle of the street.

Davin then formally introduced us. He explained to each of us who the other man was, and informed us that we had a lot of mutual friends. The beef was silly. We both understood we should be allies not enemies. After a two-minute exchange, the man and I dapped. He jumped in the car with Davin and that was that.

I walked back over to the car in rejoined my boy and the two women. On the outside I kept the ice grill so the girls could bask in my gangsta'. I knew that I was most certainly going to get a piece of ass off what had transpired in front of the girls. On the inside I exhaled. I was thankful Davin had been there to break up the situation. That nigga was big and he might have beaten me and my brother's ass in front of those girls. And besides even if I had won, I was growing tired of all the street fighting, and stock piling enemies. I was also tired of all the bumps and bruises that came with getting down in the street. My teeth still weren't all the way locked back in place.

The rest of the summer was peaceful but life never stays in a peaceful state for long. After the first month of school I found myself locked into another confrontation, but this time was different. My adversary wasn't a male or a female. My adversary was the system.

School hadn't been in session for no more than two or three weeks when I found myself day dreaming and staring out a window during an early morning class. As sat in my desk staring out the window I saw two or three cop cars pull into the school parking lot.

There was no need for me to worry or give it a second thought. I had never got into any real trouble at school and I definitely wasn't about to have any weed, dope, or weapons on me during my last year. With that many cops showing up at the school I knew somebody was in some serious trouble. It was about to go down. Today is going to be very entertaining. Some poor sucker was about to get a trip to the "clink" and it probably would be for something stupid.

After a few moments the temporary excitement died down and I drifted back into my daydream. Majority of the credits I needed for graduation were already complete. Life was good. I only had to be in school half a day to take electives. Sitting there in my desk I was thinking of everything but what the teacher was scribbling on the board when I heard my named called over the intercom. "Larry Brooks, could you please report to the front office."

Great! I didn't know what they wanted, but a break from sitting in a boring class was more than welcomed. The office was only a short walk from class. I exited the class and entered the hall way and headed toward the front office. When I got to where I could see through the glass windows of the front office I almost took off the other way. As soon as I saw them they saw me and I knew they were waiting on me by the look on their face as I made eye contact with one.

My heart started to race in fear as I entered the front office filled with cops. I hadn't done anything to my knowledge but all those police staring at me spooked the hell out of me. "Are you Larry Brooks?" The officer explained to me there had been two incidents that had transpired earlier that morning, and that I fit the description for both.

96

The first incident was an armed robbery. A gas station had been held up at gun point and the suspect was a young, light-complexioned male who drove off in a car similar to the one registered to me. The second incident was a hit and run on a mailbox in my neighborhood. The cop then informed me that they had stopped by my house and spoken with my stepdad prior to coming to the school. I was a minor, and he had given them permission to come and talk to me without a guardian present. They told me as they entered the school the robber suspect had been apprehended and that they knew the robbery had nothing to do with me. On the other hand they were going to write me a ticket for the mailbox situation. The cop informed me that he was going to arrest me but release me on the spot to myself. He said since he was doing it that way there would be no need for me to be handcuffed or take a trip downtown.

Turns out mailboxes are federal property. If you damage one and get caught you'll get charged with a felony. I was charged with a felony. Hearing the word felony scared the hell out of me. Felonies equated to disenfranchisement. I was too young to have so many opportunities blocked off from me before my life had even started. Could bumping into a mailbox with my car be that serious an offense? The irony of the situation was that I knew I was guilty. Earlier that morning I had backed into one of my neighbor's mailbox trying to turn around. I didn't think it was that serious so I got out my car and inspected the mailbox. There was no damage.

I walked back to class in disbelief. The lady of the house that called the police on me knew me personally.

She knew my name and knew where I lived. I had stopped by her house on numerous occasions to play pick up ball with her son who was two years younger than me. If here mailbox was damaged and she knew I did it why didn't she just stop by my house and speak with me or my parents to resolve the issue. Because of her over reaction I had a fist full of tickets and would be going to court over something so silly.

When I got home Timmy V couldn't wait to jump down my throat. I had never been in trouble with the law, I had never been to court before and the stress drained me. The only experience I had to draw from was from what I had seen on TV court. From what I saw on TV the courtroom was no place for a black man. Things always found a way of being blown way out of proportion when a black man stood in front of a judge. A black man steals a car and gets five years. I white man embezzles $100 million from his company and gets probation.

As soon as I walked through the door Timmy V started giving me the usual spill. Things would be different and great for me if I turned off all my thoughts and lived and breathed exactly as he instructed. I didn't lash out, I simply tuned him out. Through the years I learned how to overlook the outlandish things he said and did, but one thing he said that day was too much for me.

"Yeah, the cops came by the house and they said they could have left the ticket with me, but I told them I didn't want it. I told them to take it up to school and give it to you so you could learn a lesson."

What was this lesson he spoke of? It was beyond my understanding. Was I supposed to learn how to be traumatized by being arrested in front of my classmates in the middle of a school day? This man's thought process was backwards. In my heart I knew he loved me and meant well, but he didn't have a clue about how to love and support anybody. I realized right then if I followed anything he taught me about life I would be very successful but I also would be a miserable and lonely individual.

The whole ordeal had sucked all my energy from me. I felt sick and could barely stand or make out much of what my stepdad was saying. I politely excused myself from his nonsense. I went to my room, closed the door, and laid on the bed. I closed my eyes.

I hadn't truly feared anything to that point in my life, but I feared going into the white man's court. For a black man something as simple as bumping into a mailbox gave the system an opportunity to do whatever it chose with your life.

A few hours later I heard my mother's car pull into the garage. She was home from work and walk into the house. Before she could get her shoes off I could hear Timmy V giving my mother the details of my misfortune. From what I could hear my mother didn't say much.

The sound of her footsteps increased as she approached my bedroom. I assumed she was coming to my room to pile on to my woes. She knocked gently on my door and before she entered. She entered my room and I was still laying in the dark with my eyes closed. She flipped on the light and I didn't move. I wasn't in the mental state to deal with her coming down on me.

"Monte."

I snuck a peek at her face. She wasn't as angry as I expected. I sat up in the bed and she sat on my bed and gave me a hug. When she hugged me I felt all my frustrations trying to squeeze out threw my eyes. I kept my eyes closed. I didn't want her to see me cry.

After the hug we sorted out what had just transpired in my life. After the short talk I felt semi-calmed. My mother's strength and compassion helped me out of my minor bought of depression. She reassured everything was going to be all right. The situation wasn't as bad as it looked to my young eyes. Things had been blown out of proportion and she would walk with me through the entire process.

"That dumb bitch could have simply walked her ass down here and said something."

I was happy to hear my mother take the opposite approach from my stepdad.

"She knew enough about you to tell the police where we stayed. Tim said he went and checked the mailbox out and there wasn't any damage."

My stepdad had gone and checked the mailbox prior to me getting home from school. He added a little quick dry cement to the mailboxes foundation and it was as good as new.

The bond between my mother and I hadn't been as strong as it could have been, but my bad situation helped us take a step towards each other. Before that talk with my mother I don't remember ever sharing my troubles or confusion with anyone. I never felt comfortable enough to open up to anyone, but it felt good to share what was in my head. Why couldn't my stepdad have been there for me mentally? I didn't understand why he attempted to make me feel worse. He was a black man like I was trying to become. How could he not understand where my head was at and how could he not relate even a little bit?

Time flew and my court date came quickly. My mother took off from work that morning, and joined me on my trip to court for support as she had promised. This was one of the few times in my life I was actually truly afraid. My entire life I had been hearing black people tell horror stories about the outcome of other black people that stood before the system. I needed some support and I was beyond thankful my mother was there with me.

While we sat in the courtroom I studied the other cases that went before I was called. It didn't take long before I had an understanding of how things worked. I was shocked to find it wasn't anything like I had imagined or had seen on TV. There was no jury full of middle aged white people, and there was no audience of civilians in pews watching the proceedings like on all the court shows. There was nothing in that court room that resembled the TV shows. There was only a room full of nervous people waiting to hear their named called.

My case wasn't called until after I had been sitting in court for about three hours. I had watched at least 20 cases go before the judge. This was ga and the judge was a cliché. He was as good ol' boy as they came. He was an older white man in his mid 50's, with a sportsman's tan, and snowflake white hair. His temperament was short and agitated. He never spent much time on any one case. Most of the time, he didn't even bother to look at the defendant as they stated their business. He would read their file as they spoke and then make a quick judgment.

One case stood out more than the others. There was a young white male about the same age as me that was called before the judge. He was dressed as if he was headed to a block party as soon as he left the court room. His jeans sagged hard over his Jordans. His tee shirt was untucked and wrinkled.

The white boy was in court because he had been caught with a descent amount of weed at a football game. He had been charged with attempt to distribute on school property. The judge didn't waste much time listening to his case and sentenced the boy to six months of probation. Six months of probation didn't seem too harsh. All I had done was bump into a mail box. My case probably would be thrown out if six months of probation was all you got for selling weed at a football game.

"Larry Brooks!"

Finally, it was my turn. My confidence was high after all that I had seen before me. Dressed in brown slacks with my button upped dress shirt tucked tight into my pants in a room full of people wearing whatever should give me an edge. My church shoes and I stood before the judge, ready to clear up the minor mix-up. Every question was answered with yes sir and no sir following what I was trained to do since conception. I explained to him that I wasn't used to driving such a big car and that after hitting the mailbox, I got out and checked for possible damage before I left the scene. After I gave my short account of what happen the judge ruled quickly. He threw out the felony charge but he didn't throw out my case. Instead he dropped the charge to something lower. Then he called my sentence out. I was handed a $250 fine, he suspended my license until I completed 40 hours of community service. The judge informed me I would need to report to some country department and I would be doing beautification of the towns roads. Beautification of the town's roads meant picking up trash on the side of the street.

I left the court with a sick feeling in my stomach. How could the boy that had gotten caught with weed be handed down a lesser sentence than me? After further deliberation the situation made perfect sense. The system had treated me fairly. I was who I was and I understood the differences between me and that boy who got caught with the weed. It was all in the game. There was no use complaining. Thing had been run that way long before I came about and they would be that way after I was gone. Here I was in the beginning of my senior year and I couldn't drive anymore. On top of that I would have to waste five Saturdays giving away 40 hours of free labor.

Once I started reporting for service the time went by fast. Community service wasn't as bad as I was expecting. I reported to the waste management department and on Saturday mornings I was driven out to different areas of the city with the rest of the people in the same boat as me. We would line up on both sides of a road and pick up trash for hours at a time. We wore yellow vest to make us more visible to oncoming traffic.

The work was simple, and it was fall so the weather was decent. After the second weekend I began to become impatient. At the pace I was going it would take over a month to get my license back working only Saturdays. I only had classes half a day so if I could knock out some hours during the week I would be done in no time. Only hold up was the person supervising the community service informed me that I could work during the week but only if I could do 8-hour shifts.

After the third Saturday I overheard the guy driving the van that shuttled us to the different locations mention his boss was going on vacation starting the following Monday. That was my opportunity and I jumped on it. Knowing the man in charge would be out the office Monday I showed up to report after immediately after class the following Monday. The relieving supervisor there looked confused about what to do with me. He wasn't sure if he should allow me to work, but he eventually went ahead and okayed it. That day the van dropped off on Highway 84. It was the busiest highway in the city. It was also the route most people I knew took to get home after school.

I didn't give much thought to picking up trash on the side of 84. I was so happy that I had gotten over that could have told me I would be picking up trash on the moon and I wouldn't have cared. I was on the clock with the sanitation department from 1-5 p.m., and my shift at the PX food court didn't start until 6 p.m., so everything was working out perfectly. Time passed quickly as I cleared the trash from the side of 84. The crew I worked with were cool and not to bad to hang out with. Most of everybody was out there doing community service for minor stuff, same as I was. It only took a few minutes before I zoned out and lost myself in the work on side of that street. Then I heard the first catcall.

"Larrrrrrry!!!"

As I looked up I saw a yellow bus pass by. I caught a glimpse of one of my classmates was hanging out the bus window laughing and pointing. A few minutes later I heard a car honk its horn. I looked up to find another classmate clowning me. I threw up my arm and two fingers to acknowledge I saw him. A couple of other people drove by and tried to play me, but I wasn't ashamed of what I had to do. To hell with being ashamed, I was more concerned with getting my hours in. I was ready to get back to my life. I closed out my community service that week, paid my fine and got my license back. Fuck the system.

# JOY RIDE

This fall was different than any other I had experienced. My time wasn't dominated by sports. There were no physical and mental preparations for basketball to keep me occupied. My part-time job only had 20 hours a week available for me to work. School didn't provide much of a challenge anymore. I only had a half a day worth of classes scheduled, so I was home by 1 p.m. most afternoons with nothing to do but work out. Without sports, school, and much work, there was a large amount of time in my life that was unaccounted for. With nothing of substance to occupy my free time, I began hanging out more and more with a classmate whose schedule matched my own.

There were always rumors and whispers about my homeboy's character. I brushed off the down talking of my homeboy and put it into the category of hating. I didn't have any problems with hanging with my homeboy, but from time to time, I would be questioned why I was so closely associated with someone of questionable character. He was constantly ridiculed about being a pretty boy or about being soft. I didn't concern myself with the hating. Besides, I had my own haters. I figured the hate for my man stemmed from his family coming across as uppity. Unlike most of our peers, his parents choose to spend a little more of their disposable income on providing him with above-average apparel. He was always dressed in the latest fashion, and his shoe game was by far the best in the school. Our high school was small and full of children from working-class homes with working-class lifestyles. The false perception of him being uppity made him a constant target of hate.

Knowing that jealousy was the foundation for majority of the resentment my friend encountered, I didn't put any stock in the negative feedback I received for dealing with him. I didn't buy into all the negative talk about my friend because I had seen a different side of his character. A few years before, a couple of other guys and I were playing pickup basketball games outside of my friend's home. I was attempting to play 21 in some beat-up running shoes, and it wasn't happening for me. After a few incidences of me almost breaking my ankle my friend disappeared and reappeared with a pair of Jordans. The shoes looked as if they had only been worn a few times. I had never owned a pair Jordans or even tried on a pair. When I was handed the shoes I wasn't sure about the idea of playing pickup basketball in a new pair of Jordans. That made absolutely no sense to me. I would have preferred to take them home and wear them to school Monday morning. After assuring me it was no big deal, I put on the shoes and rejoined the pickup game. Playing hard was no longer an option. There was no way I was going to scuff those shoes. After the game I made an attempt to return the shoes, but he told me to hold on to them. He informed me that he would get them back from me when he needed them, but he never asked for or mentioned the shoes again.

One Friday night my friend and I were riding and listening to Pac and No Limit in his compact car. Since there was no mall or hotspot to cruise, we rode through different neighborhoods in town trying to get lucky and stumble on some loose girls to flirt with. On this night in particular things went a little different. My friend turned off Highway 84 and pulled his compact car into a hotel parking lot near the football stadium. Before I could ask him what he was doing he told me he had something he wanted to show me.

Clueless as to what he could possibly have to show me in a hotel parking lot, I just went alone with the plan. We drove through the parking lot and parked in the back of the hotel where there was only one other car parked. We pulled up next to the car and sat for a second, and he didn't say anything. He just stared at the car we had just parked beside. The car next to us was a new Lexus and was completely covered with at least two weeks' worth of dust. The dust covered the car evenly in one thick layer. It was easy to tell the car had been sitting still for a minute.

"So what do you think?"

I answered him back, "think about what, nigga? What in the hell are you talking about?"

"What do you think about my car?"

He smirked and looked at the Lexus and nodded. We jumped out of the car, and he pulled out a key and unlocked both the doors. I sat in the passenger seat, and he jumped in the driver's seat.

"How did you pull this shit off?"

He never did give me a straight answer. He gave me the run around and gave me some half-gangsta' answer stating that he'd "made a move." That answer was good enough for me. I didn't care, and I didn't need to know exactly how he came about the car. The excitement of getting ready to go for a joyride in a Lexus was good enough for me.

My riding partner popped the trunk on his compact car and took out a license plate he had stolen. He swapped the plate on the Lexus with the one he had stolen and threw the old plate in the trunk of his compact car. We left his car there and took off in the Lexus. Our first destination was to pick up two other boys, Fernando and Big Bob, to go joyriding with us. After Fernando and Big Bob jumped in the car we left Hinesville and headed to Savannah. Driving the car in Hinesville was out of the question. The Lexus would have attracted too much attention in the small town, and we probably would have been locked up within the hour.

We took back roads behind Ft. Stewart to avoid driving through Hinesville and made a beeline to Savannah. I figured if we made it out of Hinesville in the car we would be in the clear. I quietly tightened the drawstring on my sweatpants and the laces in my shoes. If we got pulled over, I was committed to making a run for it. My nerves didn't settle down until Hinesville and Ft. Stewart were in the rearview mirror.

We made it to Savannah without any trouble and decided to cruise the streets for a couple of hours. We swapped drivers every 20 minutes or so. The adrenaline rush was off the charts. We would pull into to any gas station and fast food restaurant parking lots trying to be seen driving the Lexus. If we saw any young girls, we made sure to find away to let them see us in the car. We pulled up beside girls and talked out the window like we were kingpins. It felt as if all eyes were on us.

After everyone had their turn driving the wheel was offered to me. I took the wheel for a short time, but I didn't drive the car long before I passed it off to someone else. I wasn't comfortable driving in the city. My license had only been reinstated for less than a month, and I wasn't willing to be in the driver's seat if we got pulled over.

After a few hours of cruising, we headed back to country. We dropped the other two boys off first then headed back to the hotel to swap out the cars. After we got back to the hotel, I jumped in his car and followed him to another hotel to park the Lexus. It had been sitting in the hotel parking lot for too long; it was time to move it elsewhere. After we relocated the Lexus, he dropped me off at home. Before I went inside, I stood still and exhaled because I was happy we didn't get caught in that stolen car. I also had a thought about my friend: People called him soft, but they didn't know shit about him. Folks had him all wrong.

After that one night of joyriding, I never laid eyes on that Lexus again. We never spoke about the car, and I didn't bother to ask about it. It was a one-night love affair for me because riding around in dirty cars wasn't something I wanted to make a habit of doing.

A few weeks later I found myself in familiar territory. We were again cruising through town in my friend's compact car looking for something to get into. The night was slow and there wasn't much happening. After an hour of wasting gas we found ourselves directionless at a red light. We had been riding in silence listening to the radio for the past few minutes. As we sat waiting at the long light, the silence was broken when my friend asked me a question that aroused my curiosity. He asked me if I was interested in making some fast money. A few weeks back I would have brushed off a question like that coming from him, but I had to take him seriously after the joyride in the Lexus. I didn't ask any questions and agreed to the proposition without much thought. I wanted to know what else this guy had hidden up his sleeve.

# REDEMPTION

It was close to 2 a.m., so there were few cars on the streets with us. We rode through the empty streets, and I listened as he gave me a short rundown of how we were about to make some quick money. The discussion ended. Minutes later we pulled into a quiet neighborhood and slowly drove through it. We decided it was what we had been looking for, so we left to park his car in a nearby apartment complex. As we made our way back to the neighborhood, my heart felt like it was about to jump out of my chest. Every few houses we would spot a car worth peeking into, and one of us would run up and look inside. It took about five minutes to find a car worth entering.

He crouched beside the car and signaled me over to peek into the driver's window to take a look for myself. He had found a jackpot. Inside the car was a high-end Alpine tape player and matching equalizer in the deck. Common sense told us if the deck was loaded then there had to be speakers and an amp we couldn't see in the back of the car. We walked away from the car to make sure we hadn't set off any alarms and made our way up the street. After confirming we had the clear, we circled back to the car.

As we approached the car my friend reached into his back pocket and pulled out a spark plug. I continued to walk up the block past the car to play lookout. He ran past the car and threw the spark plug into the window like a baseball. The glass shattered into a million pieces when the spark plug hit it, but it didn't fall to the ground. In that moment, the sound of the spark plug against the glass seemed like the loudest noise I had ever heard in my life. It was the middle of the night with nothing to drown out the sound of the window shattering. That loud pop had to have awakened everybody in the house and the surrounding neighbors. I just knew the gig was up, so I took off and started to run up the street. I had gotten about 15 yards away before I even considered looking back to see if my accomplice was following me.

I glanced back to see my friend was motioning for me to return. I started back toward the car that had just had its window broken. As I was making my way back to the car I could see he was putting his arm into the hole made by the spark plug. The loud noise that spooked me—that I was sure everybody within half a block had heard—hadn't caused a stir. No lights in any houses turned on. No doors flung open. I had been wrong. Either no one had heard or been alarmed enough by the noise to see what was happening. I had run off and made myself look like a bitch for nothing.

By time I crept back over to the car he had already entered the vehicle and seemed to have completely kept his composure. Throughout our dealings I had never been in awe of my friend. He seemed to never excel or posses any particular skill I considered of importance. But in the car he was polished. Inside that car picking it apart he was in his element, and I found myself admiring skills. He was a professional and even carried a black bag full of tools which he rambled through as he worked.

Time sat still as I sat on the outside of the car watching. It felt as if he was pulling and yanking at wires for 30 minutes. I grew more and more impatient as each minute passed.

"What the hell is taking you so long? Let's make a move."

He whispered back at me, "Give me a few more seconds. I'm trying to get this amp, but it's bolted to the floor under the passenger seat, so I can't get at it good."

"Fuck that amp! Let's go."

As I sat waiting for the heist to end, the scene from the movie *South Central,* when the boy gets shot with a shotgun while trying to steal a car radio, replayed in my head. I was more than ready break camp. A few more minutes passed before the driver's door opened. He got out with the amp under his arm and the tape deck and equalizer stuffed in his hoodie. I was excited that we pulled off a good heist, but he had taken too much time for my liking.

He was also little too cool about it all and walking too slowly for me. I started a light jog back to our getaway ride. When we were finally back in the car he immediately unleashed the jokes. To him, it was hilarious that I had been spooked and dashed off when the spark plug hit the window. He had finally seen me show some weakness and made sure to exploit it through humor. I did find it a bit funny in hindsight, but only because we had gotten away clean.

The next day he brought some of the stolen goods to school to sell. It didn't take long to move the goods. He gave a couple dope boys a peek at our loot, and it was as good as sold. Within an hour he made close to $250. The only problem with the sale was he tried to leave me in the dark. It was by chance that I found out he brought the goods to school and had sold them before 2nd period started. The local dope boy who had scored the goods and I were cool, so he mentioned the purchase to me. The dope boy was excited because he knew the tape deck by itself was valued at about $400. Fortunately for me, he felt the need to brag about his good fortune.

I played the role as lookout and had put my freedom on the line just as much as he did during the score. If we would have gotten caught, we both would have suffered the same fate. My friend had done the most of the work and deserved most of the profit. I wasn't expecting a 50/50 split, but I was expecting compensation. I didn't see or hear from my friend at all that day. The next day we crossed paths in the high school hallway, and I didn't waste too much time before I asked him about my share of the profit. That's when I got my first taste of his true character.

"Look man, I did all the work," he said.

I should have gone with my first thought and knocked his front teeth down his throat. I hadn't asked him for an even split, but the proper thing to do would have been to slide me $50 of the $250. I was steaming on the inside. This nigga had asked me to go on a score with him and put my freedom on the line, and all he could say to me was "I did all the work"? He knew I was angry, but I ended the conversation with a simple "Ok, I understand."

The thoughts of having shown weakness during the heist and then not being compensated left me sleepless at night. In my mind, my testicles were up for questioning. The next weekend after work I invited him to take a ride with me. I didn't tell him where we going and we just rode in silence. I drove around for a few hours killing time waiting for midnight. I was driving around, casing and searching for what I wanted to see.

During the cruising I had spotted a couple of vehicles I wanted to investigate. A little after midnight I parked my '83 Pontiac Bonneville, and we made our way toward a couple prospects. The first car window I looked through had a Kenwood tape deck. That was good enough for me. That week had been long, and my mind had started feeding on itself. The fear I had during the first heist was nonexistent. Trying to make a quick dollar was nonexistent in my mind as well. This wasn't about the thrill or even about the car stereo; this was about something different. This was about redemption.

I did a brief check to make sure the area was clear for me to proceed with what I had come to do. Without any warning or much thought, I hurled the spark plug I had purchased a few days earlier into the window. Without hesitation I pulled my fist into my sweat shirt sleeve and punched the car window to widen the hole the spark plug made. In my haste, I had forgotten to grab the screw driver and wire cutters I had brought along with me from the car. The only tool I had on me was the pocket blade I carried.

As I sat in the driver's seat I checked the car for anything extra I could take before I tried to snatch out the tape deck. There wasn't anything extra to be had. I hadn't stumbled on a mother lode like my friend had found during the last outing, but at least there was a brand new Kenwood tape deck staring at me. As I sat in the car I realized all my fear wasn't gone, and I wanted to be in and out as fast as possible.

I shoved my knife between the tape deck and the housing unit. I pried out the tape deck just enough to get a grip on it with my hand. This wasn't my car, and I wasn't concerned with making a cosmetically appeasing heist. I got a good enough grip and yanked the Kenwood out as hard as I could. Unfortunately, I yanked half the dash out with the tape deck. I took my razor sharp knife and slashed the wires and excited the car as quickly as I had entered.

With the radio tucked under sweatshirt, I was ready to flee the scene. I scanned the cars in the vicinity looking for my partner in crime. I spotted my counterpart sitting in a Jeep Wrangler. There had been no windows for him to bust, just plastic to cut. He was seated in the front seat scrambling through the compartments. I made eye contact with him and signaled to him that I was ready to leave. He gave me a look back as if he needed more time. I was leaving anyway. Luckily for him he caught on that I was leaving with or without him. If he would have taken any longer than two minutes to make it back to my car, he would have been walking home that night.

# BROTHER'S KEEPER

Breaking into cars delivered an adrenaline rush with no equal in my world, but the risk outweighed the reward tenfold. A week after taking my first car stereo with my partner I went out and pulled off another theft by myself. As I drove away from the scene I saw at least four or five cops in patrol cars driving their beats. After careful consideration I decided early retirement from the smash-and-grab business was best for my future.

After I returned home from my first and only solo heist, I found all the doors to the house dead bolted and chain locked. Typical Friday. Timmy V locked the doors with chains around 11:30 p.m. every time I went out. He did it purposely so I would have to ring the doorbell. He wanted to track and micro management my movements. I was 17, had a job, and paid for all my own expenses under his roof. I wasn't interested in playing his game of tracking me, so I simply didn't participate. To circumvent ringing the doorbell and putting a timestamp on my coming and going, I knocked on my brother's window for entry when I came home after lockdown.

After a few taps on his window, Gene would unlock the back door and turn off the alarm for me to enter the house undetected. This would drive Timmy V insane, and he would threaten us with punishment. I would be out of that house in less than six months, so I tuned out Timmy V's micromanagement and outlandish talk.

My brother would usually go back to his room and continue on with his business after helping me gain entry into the house. For some reason, he unexpectedly decided to enter my room unannounced to talk that night. My mother didn't allow locked doors in her house, but no one ever came into my room without knocking. When he entered into my room I had just laid both of my stolen car stereos on the bed. He caught me off guard. My brother was only a year younger than me and wasn't a snitch, so I didn't bother trying to make up a lie to tell him. He immediately shut the door and asked me what I was up to. I didn't glorify what I had been doing. I actually tried to do my best to deter my brother from ever attempting to run the same hustle by telling him it was a waste of time. Breaking into cars was too risky for such a small payoff.

Even though Gene was only a year younger, he still looked to me for leadership. My actions made strong impressions on him, and he tended to follow my lead. He was a good solider as long as he had good leadership. During our talk I made a point to stress how I was finished and that it was stupid that I even tried the hustle. Gene didn't say much, and I was comfortable that he got the message.

My '83 Pontiac Bonneville was still equipped with a factory radio and due for an upgrade. It took a couple of hours and multiple trips to the electronic store, but I finally managed to get one of the stolen tape decks installed. Before the installation of the tape deck I wasn't overly enthused with my '83. I didn't care for the car because Timmy V had taken the money I left in his care while I was in Texas for the summer and purchased the car without my input. He went half on the car for me, so I couldn't really complain. He added $1,000 to match the $1,000 I left behind. I was very thankful for the gesture, but I didn't appreciate someone spending my money without giving me any say. After the installation was complete I immediately went out and bought a portable CD player with a car adapter.

After my '83 was equipped with a decent sound system, my appreciation for the car increased tenfold. My new favorite pastime was driving around town solo. I would blast DJ Screw, Tela, Scarface, UGK and Pac while I rode around town with my all four windows down.

It had been over a week since the last heist, and I hadn't seen my partner outside of school. I wasn't concerned with hanging out as much anymore. I had sound in my car, and I was still salty about how he had conducted business after the first theft.

It was a few days later, and I was about to head home after my shift as a janitor at the PX on Ft. Stewart. After a few hours of cleaning dirty bathrooms and mopping floors the only thing on my mind was taking a shower and get ready for a Friday night of cruising. As I pulled into my subdivision, I could immediately sense there was something different in the air. I hadn't gotten both feet out of my car before Leonard rode up to my car on a bike.

"Say, bruh, I don't know what happened, but your brother is in the police car up the street."

As he spoke my heart sank into my stomach. I jumped on the handle bars and he paddled me around the block to where two police cars were parked with their lights flashing. I approached the cars and got a glimpse of my 15-year-old brother sitting in the back of one of the cruisers, cuffed and looking like he had seen a ghost. In the other cruiser was my brother's best friend, Tré, who was cuffed and looking just as scared. My heart sank even further. What could my brother have possibly done?

Leonard stopped the bike about 15 yards from the police cruisers. I jumped off the handle bars and walked up to the side of the cruiser housing my brother. As I stared through the glass at him, he gave me a look of desperation and started mumbling.

"Bruh, I swear! I didn't do anything. I don't know why they're fucking with me!"

I lost myself in the moment and forgot I was dealing with the police. Gene was my brother, and it was my job to protect him by any means. Before I could think things through my instincts took over. I proceeded to talk loudly to the cops in the fashion I had seen social activists do on the documentaries from the '70s. I demanded to know why my brother was in the backseat. I learned a quick lesson: This wasn't the 70s, and there were no TV cameras took keep the cops off my ass. Before I could get a complete four sentences out of my mouth, I was being choked out by one of the cops involved.

Luckily for me the partner of the cop choking me possessed a little more compassion and understanding for what I was going through. Before the cop could do any real damage twisting my arm and neck his partner blurted out, "Hey get off that kid."

The cop released me, and my breath returned slowly. My willingness to aggress the cops didn't. The cop that saved my neck politely asked Leonard and me to clear the scene and let them do their job. Leonard offered to give me a bike ride back home, but I declined. My house was less than a block away, and I needed time to think.

I walked into the house to find my mother and Timmy V already set to make the trip down to the police station. The cops had been to the house and spoken with my parents. They informed me of what the cops told them after we'd gotten in the car.

My brother and Tré had broken into a car a block away from where we lived. While they were breaking into the car, the owner was in the house watching the entire time from a window. They were under the impression that the owner had taken another vehicle to work. Obviously, they didn't get the memo that he changed up his routine. When the cops arrived they were still sitting in the car trying to snatch the radio. My brother being jumped out the car, left the cops, his buddy, and his shoes long behind. Tré tried to run but got scared and stopped running to hide in a doghouse not too far from the scene. The cops found Tré in the doghouse. The irony of their failed robbery was the man they tried to rob was familiar with both of them. My brother and Tré were associates of his son. After they got away he told the cops exactly where my brother lived so they stopped by the house and picked him up a few minutes after he fled.

My mother cried as she told me the story, and my stomach turned over again and again. I wasn't sure if I was more upset with my brother or myself. I was very aware my brother had the habit of mimicking my behavior, but I had ordered him not to attempt this hustle. It had only been a week or less since the talk in my room, and he had already managed to get himself arrested.

I always had a certain level of trust for my brother because we were family, but throughout his case and community service he showed me something new. My brother and Tré never mentioned me or spoke a word on where they came up with the idea to break into the car. To this very day over 15 years later they never mentioned it to me, not even in jest.

Needless to say conscious ate at me as I watched them go through the courts. Those two young boys looked to me for guidance, and I guided them right into the system.

# READY TO FLY

Hanging out was the last thing I wanted to do after the situation with my brother. I kept to myself for a few weeks. I hung around the house and didn't stray too far from my neighborhood. Sometimes when I was home my mother would confide in me. She was under the impression that I was a good source of strength, and that I managed to keep myself pointed in the right direction. My mother was stressing out trying to figure how to not let my brother head any further down his current path. He was struggling with school before the incident and managed to land himself in the legal system. It doesn't take much to derail a young, black male's future, and she was well aware how easy things take a turn from bad to worse. I knew my brother would be ok. I wanted to tell her not to worry. He was just following my bad choices like a dumb little brother. I wanted to tell her that it was more my fault than his because I had implanted the idea, but I didn't have the courage. Luckily, my brother did bounce back to the straight path. After a couple hundred hours of community service he was back to his life. Things slowly went back to normal.

My school year was quickly coming to a close and in a few months, I would graduate high school. A month after graduation I would turn18. I would be on my own. I would be a man in the eyes of the world.

Until the year of '96 there had never been a question in my mind about what I wanted out my life. Everything was crystal clear: I would go to a small college and play basketball, and the rest would take care of itself. Things hadn't worked out the way I planned. Away from the watchful eye of most people that knew me, I was becoming more like the street thugs I grew up around than the better version of D-Ray that I had envisioned. My secret actions had led me to a fork in the road of my life. Would my future hold prison or college?

Anticipation of the great unknown outside of the nest generated excitement within me. Each passing day felt like a day closer to freedom. Every day passing was one less day I would have to live under the rules of another man. The nest had become too restricting. I was ready to fly.

# A THOUSAND DEATHS

Before I flew the coop there was one last lesson that I needed to learn. I learned it well. My robbing partner and I gradually began to cruise the streets together again on occasion, but I slowed down the risky behavior. We didn't hang daily, or even weekly, anymore, but it was rare if we went two whole weeks without cruising. Most of my other associates were busy playing sports or trying to spend as much time as possible being in love with one girl. Both of our options were limited, so we ended up hanging out whether we liked it or not.

We were in the country so there wasn't much to do outside of driving the streets unless there was a sporting event. There wasn't anything bigger or better than a high school basketball game in Hinesville. A basketball game on a Friday night would infuse the town with life.

One Friday night in particular I met my riding partner in the Kroger parking lot about a half a mile from Checkers. I parked my car and jumped in the car with my boy. My riding partner and I were both too cool to take a seat in the gym and watch a game with the rest of town. We wouldn't go inside, but we would parking lot pimp with the best of them.

The night was going no different than any other. We were engaged in our normal routine: cruising the town in his car burning gas and blasting his system. The system in my car had been upgraded through my theft, but it was still basic. His stereo system was a monster, so his car was better suited for drawing attention when we pulled into a parking lot. We drove around for at least an hour buying time until the game let out and filled the fast food restaurant parking lots with teens. After we were sure the game let out and the lots should be full, we headed to McDonald's. We pulled into the McDonald's parking lot blasting the recently deceased Tupac's *Makevelli*.

He was very particular about his sound system and overtly concerned about quality. The system wasn't simply loud and trunk rattling like what you typically heard coming out of the box Chevy's around town. He had gone so far as to put rubber stoppers on all the screws in the trunk and on his license plate to limit the rattling. The speakers and amps in his car were all custom mounted and professionally installed. Needless to say his tape deck was top-of-the-line and put on a light show in his car that could be seen from the outside as he drove by.

When we pulled into a parking lot the sound coming from his car forced the crowds in the parking lot to turn our way to see who was coming through. Before we would enter a parking lot swarming with teens I would lean back the seat very far. We would drive through a parking lot and both pretend as if we didn't notice all the eyes turning toward us. Part of the parking lot pimping game was being cool and not acknowledging that you were the center of attention. It had to look natural. It was all part of the game. It didn't take much to generate hate towards you we you were in a small town where people didn't have much. If other teen boys frowned at us when we pulled up that confirmed we were on point. That meant we were winning.

The first spot we hit was slow. There wasn't much going on in the McDonald's parking lot so we headed down 84 looking for a better scene. I could see the parking lot of Checkers was packed from a distance, so we turned off 84 into Checkers and did a couple of slow laps in the parking lot. Checkers was packed, but there weren't many people in the parking lot that we recognized. Our school's basketball team didn't have a game that particular Friday. Our cross-town rival, Bradwell Institute, had played a home game that night instead. All the he hangout spots were filled with teenagers from that high school with a few familiar faces from our high school sprinkled here and there.

We drove through the parking lot with the windows down allowing the loud, crisp music to draw the eyes of the crowd. When we were satisfied with the attention gained by driving through the parking lot we parked and set up shop. There were a few young girls walking around and mingling, but not enough for every male who wanted one. The ratio was four or five hardheaded, teenage boys to every young female. So many men competing for so few females was a testosterone-charged bomb waiting to explode. There was no reason to get out the car for such few available females, so we sat in the car, listened to music, and watched the scene unfold.

There wasn't anything special about the scene at the parking lot. It seemed to be a typical teenage gathering.

"You want anything? I'm about to go grab a burger," my partner asked.

"Naw, I'm good." I declined his offer and stayed seated in the car. I went about my business of watching the crowd and listening to music. We were parked about 30 yards from the restaurant, and the car was positioned at an angle that gave us sight of every person coming and going. We parked so we couldn't be blocked in, and we didn't want to be too close to all the action.

I watched as my friend slowly made his way across the parking lot. He walked slowly with an air of coolness. There were people watching because we had just pulled into the parking lot like we thought we were royalty. He approached the walkup order window with a slow pimp stroll. As he eased across the parking lot, I got a glimpse of a Suburban somewhat speeding toward him from his right. He was already in the middle of where the truck was headed before my friend noticed the truck headed right for him. He was a pedestrian, so he had the right of way, but those rules don't apply unless the driver of the vehicle chooses to follow them. I didn't think anything of it, because I assumed the truck would slow up and let him finish walking across the parking lot. I was wrong. The driver did the opposite of what was expected. The truck sped up and forced my homeboy to dive out of the way to prevent being struck.

I consider the normal reaction to being almost run over to be shock or anger, but my homeboy quickly gathered himself. He stood up straight and through his hands in the air as if to ask, "What the fuck?" That's when the proverbial shit hit fan. Almost simultaneously as he through his hands up the brake lights on the truck illuminated. The driver had slammed on the brakes and thrown the truck in park. All the doors on the truck seemed to open at once. Five young thugs jumped out the truck and quickly formed a semi-circle around my friend. I couldn't see his face because his back was to me, but I could sense the fear in his body language.

The driver of the truck stepped up close to my friend. Only a few words were spoken before he drew back his right hand. Before I could gather my thoughts the driver delivered a slap to my friend's face that twisted his head halfway around. Without a second thought I jumped out of the car and ran toward the conflict. The time from the truck stopping to the slap couldn't have been more than 30 seconds. Things seemed to slow down to a crawl at that point, and I could see everything unfold as if someone had pressed a slow-motion button.

Seeing five of them on two of us told me things weren't in our favor, but he was my friend. As a true friend I was obligated to stand in there, win or lose, with him. If he had to take an ass whipping, then I had to take an ass whipping. At least this way we could split the ass whipping between us.

Fear froze my partner like ice. He got slapped and didn't make an attempt to defend himself or strike back. He stood there after the slap and stared at his feet. I wasn't close enough to hear what was being said, but it looked as if my friend was being disciplined by his father. The guy who had just done the slapping was pointing his finger in my friend's face and giving him the dos and don'ts of his territory.

After running through the parking lot around some cars and through some bushes, I finally made it to the confrontation. I didn't waste time and ran right up to the situation and took position next to my friend. I lined myself and stood shoulder to shoulder with him. We both faced off against the five. My sudden presence interrupted the lecture my friend was receiving, and the slapper stopped talking. There was no point in me saying anything because the first blow had already been thrown. I immediately put my hands up. I was ready to fight beside my friend.

I squared up on all five as best I could. I scanned them and picked out the smallest guy of the group and focused in on him. He wasn't that much bigger than me. The plan was to get in close and wrap him up. If I went down to the ground, he was going with me. If I was going to get stomped, he would get stomped.

Before engaging, I glanced to my side to see if my partner was ready to go war. I couldn't believe what I saw: nothing! He wasn't there. All I saw was a glimpse of him running back in the direction I had come. I was so focused on the five guys in front of me that I hadn't notice him leave. Did I really just run into a fight to help this coward and end up alone against five thugs?

My options flashed before my eyes. I only had two. The first option was to turn and run same as my partner had done, but that would be the move of a coward. The second option was to stay and fight five-on-one. That would be the choice of a fool. The last option was to summon up the courage to attempt to broker a peaceful deal, if possible. I didn't realize right away that a third option existed. I chose what came naturally.

A solider only dies once. I swung like it would be the last punch I would ever throw. Being that I was seriously outnumbered, there was a chance it might be. I pummeled the guy who had done the slapping. He stumbled back toward the truck behind him. I knew what would happen after I threw the punch, but I made the choice to go down swinging. After I hit the first guy things got ugly for me, and they got ugly very fast. I ended up surrounded. I was taking punches from every angle. My only thought was maintaining my feet, and I was doing everything in my power to not go to the ground. Going down meant getting stomped. Getting stomped increased the possibility of getting seriously injured, or worse.

I had heard too many stories about people getting stomped into a bloody mess, getting facial bones fractured, and even getting killed by gangs after hitting the ground. The thought of what could happen on the ground kept me on my feet through the barrage of punches. After a minute or so my nightmare came to fruition. Because the five men couldn't get me down with hands, they attacked me from a different angle.

It happened so fast that there was nothing I could do. I assumed the fetal position and prayed they showed mercy. After standing tall and doing the best I could, suddenly, I was foot swept from behind. My feet were now located where my hands once were, and my hands were now where my feet had been. Would tonight be the night I died in the street in front of a bunch of strangers? Was this going to be the way it all ended for me? Until that point in my life I had never given my own death much thought.

The boots started raining down on me like hail from the heavens. All I could manage to do was ball up as tight as possible. I tucked my head as best I could into my chest and covered my face. I could feel the boots kicking and stomping me but, I don't remember feeling any pain. I was lying on the ground getting stomped when I drifted off into deep thought. Was I wrong to run to my friend's aid? Was this how the universe rewarded my courage? As suddenly as it had started the stomping stopped. I didn't move because I was sure the stomping would begin again as soon as I untucked my body.

My eyes were still closed and I was still in the fetal when I felt someone pull me off the ground. The arms stood me on my feet.

"Get up little nigga, we got ya!"

I opened my eyes and it was Big Bob. I barely knew this cat, but he and a couple of his boys had come to my rescue. He had been the fourth guy riding in that stolen Lexus with my friend, Fernando, and me. We had also played ball a few times when we were younger, but I didn't know him well enough to consider him an ally. Big Bob and a couple of his friends had come to my rescue and tossed the five off me while I was getting stomped.

I was back on my feet and riding off adrenaline. I couldn't feel the pain of what had just happen to me; what I was feeling was rage. Somebody would pay for the beating that had been given to me. The first one of the five thugs I laid eyes on would get everything I had. I spotted one, then he spotted me, and our eyes locked. I saw the same look in his eyes that I had possessed when Chris Ford got up off the ground to fight me after I had beaten him with the hammer. It was fear. I was knocked down, stomped on, but I wasn't finished. I still had plenty fight left. I rushed him with everything I had, both hands swinging.

His fear locked him up and he couldn't find the courage to throw back a punch. I punched him in the face repeatedly until the punches forced him to go to the ground. He covered up, but I kept punching him. My heart was ice. I wanted to destroy him like they had tried to destroy me. Before I could finish him with a good stomping I heard the universal signal to break camp.

"Fuck these niggas; I'm going to get my pistol."

The words came from the mouth of one of the five. I wasn't going to pretend I wasn't afraid of getting shot. I gave the punk on the ground beneath me one last kick to the ribs and fled down Highway 84 on foot. I almost got hit by a car as I crossed over the highway trying run away, but I stood a better chance against traffic than against bullets. I never looked back to see if I was being followed as I ran. I also never got a chance to thank Big Bob and his friends for coming to my rescue.

I stopped running after I felt safe, and my adrenaline wore off. I could now feel the pains of what my body had just been through. My shirt was half torn off, my jeans were scuffed, and there were boot imprints covering my body. I glanced over my arms and gazed at the red swollen imprints of the bottom of timberlands up and down both my forearms.

I approached Kroger the first thing I saw was my MIA partner parked right next to my car. I pretended I didn't see him and tried to make it to my car door without conversation. He approached me staring as if he was looking at a ghost.

Before he could say anything I asked, "What happened to you? Why did you run?"

He looked me right in the eyes, smirked, and said, "I didn't ask you to help me; that became your fight."

I couldn't reply because I felt a rage starting to build. My first thought was to give him a fight right there, but two things stopped me. My left shoulder felt as if it was partially dislocated from getting stomped, and I couldn't fault him for being afraid. He hadn't been built like me.

I brushed past him, got in my car, and headed down 84 toward my home. I slowly leaned my seat back until I was almost on the back seat. I let down all four windows. I turned up my music and let the wind brush against my face as I drifted off into thought while I drove.

Honor illuminated me. I knew my counterpart wouldn't sleep well that night. The coward would have to go into some dark places in his mind. He would have to relive running from that fight a thousand times. He would have to die a thousand times. My body was bruised and battered, but I rode home with the honor of a gladiator who had stood tall in the arena. I had survived another battle. I had survived '96.